HOW CAN I
HEAR GOD?

GILLIAN PEALL

HOW CAN I
HEAR GOD?

SCRIPTURE UNION

Scripture Union, 207–209 Queensway, Bletchley, MK2 2EB, England.

© Gillian Peall 1999

First published 1999

ISBN 1 85999 293 5

Unless otherwise attributed, Scriptures are taken from the Holy Bible, New International Version. Copyright © 1973, 1978, 1984 by International Bible Society. Anglicisation copyright © 1979, 1984, 1989. Used by permission of Hodder and Stoughton Limited.

British Library Cataloguing-in-Publication Data
A catalogue record for this book is available from the British Library.

Cover design by Mark Carpenter Design Consultants.
Printed and bound in Great Britain by Cox & Wyman, Reading, Berkshire.

CONTENTS

ACKNOWLEDGEMENTS

I would like to thank Steve and Teresa, and all the members of the Christian Life Fellowship who loved me, prayed for me, supported me and put up with me while I wrote this book. Without them it would never have seen the light of day!

I would also like to thank all those who so willingly shared their experiences of hearing God so that I could put them in the book. Every single account is true, but some of the names have been changed. Thanks, too, to Josephine Campbell at Scripture Union, for all her hard work and help.

Lastly, I want to say 'thank you' to Sue and Daran, my daughter and son-in-law, for their insight, encouragement, helpful criticism and expertise.

Chapter 1

A GOD WHO SPEAKS

The first time I ever heard God speak to me I nearly jumped out of my skin.

I was walking my dog one morning and asking God to show me how he wanted me to serve him. I had only been a Christian a month or so, and in my naïvety and arrogance I was saying in effect, 'Well, here I am, Lord. What do you want me to do? How do you want me to change the world?'

Various friends had lent me those testimony books where the scenario goes as follows. Wife becomes a Christian. Within a couple of weeks the husband is either so overcome by the change in his wife – or he picks up her Bible by accident – that he too gives his life to Christ. They both immediately begin a ministry among the local drop-outs/drug addicts, planting and pastoring a church based in a disused warehouse/nightclub. I think I rather expected God to organise something similar for me! I was very shaken, therefore, when I heard a booming voice behind me saying just three words: 'READ THE BIBLE!'

I turned round to see who it was, wondering for a moment if I had prayed out loud as I walked along.

But the road was totally deserted. Someone from my home group lived down a nearby cul-de-sac, and I half expected to see him leaning out of his window, calling to me. I was rooted to the spot when I realised that I had heard *God* speak. I never had a moment's doubt that it was God. I *knew*, and I still know, that the voice I'd heard was his voice.

I was also rather disappointed. I wanted a ministry, not a lot of homework! In fact, it was the best advice I, or any Christian, could receive. Well, it would be, wouldn't it? I do believe that God had to shout at me because my ears and mind were blocked by my own arrogance and pride. Maybe the closer and more open we are to God, the softer he speaks to us.

Only through the Bible?

It was some time before I realised that not everyone hears God speak aloud. At first I didn't think to mention it to anyone else, as I thought it happened to everyone! When I did talk about what I'd heard, I was gently but firmly told that today the only way God speaks to Christians is through reading the Bible.

I was bewildered and saddened by this, partly because I obviously wasn't believed but also because I felt that this was not entirely true. It seemed to imply that it was unnecessary to hear God speaking personally to me: we have the Bible and that should be enough. A 'Manual for life' and 'Handbook for living' it is called, and of course it is. But while God can and does speak to us through the Bible into our individual circumstances, the Bible itself is more like a general guide to the principles of godly living. For example, the Bible is quite clear that God expects us to be good stewards of the money he gives us, and many believe that it is right to tithe our incomes. But is this before or after tax? The apostle James states that true religion means looking after widows and orphans (James 1:27), but this doesn't altogether help us when we are trying to decide which charity to make a donation to. Starving widows and orphans? Sick, blind or maimed widows and orphans? What about starving families, persecuted Christians and all the other needs today's world throws at us? We need to understand that while James is talking about the underprivileged and unsupported in the first century, we can draw from his words principles on which we can base our decision as to where our money should go in our own time; and then we can ask God for specific guidance.

'Is it really important that I hear God? If I go to church on Sunday and do my best to live a good life, isn't that enough?' Well, no, it isn't. God's instructions to me, 'Read the Bible', could have been directed at any new Christian. We cannot build solid foundations for our faith unless we know what God says in his word.

'OK, I go to church and I read the Bible (perhaps not as often as I should, but I lead a busy life). Isn't *that* enough?' Lots of Christians would probably say yes to that, but I think they are missing a vital element in their Christian life. A relationship with someone, by definition, includes communication. When communication between a husband and wife has stopped, we say the relationship has broken down. If a daughter stops writing or telephoning her aged and distant widowed mother, then there is no real relationship between them, even though they are related by blood. The aged mother could say, quite truthfully, 'My daughter has nothing to do with me now.'

Some of the saddest people around today are those we call 'stalkers', especially those who follow famous media or pop stars. Convinced that the star reciprocates their adoration, they write or telephone them and dog their footsteps. Some are even convinced that their 'love' is returned and that marriage is perfectly possible. But the plain fact is, there is no relationship. Communication does not exist, as real communication must be two-way. One-way communication is dead and lifeless, like junk mail.

Our relationship with God needs to be two-way for it to be vibrant, life-enhancing and real. When we pray, or just talk to God, we need to make sure that we are hearing the other side of the conversation. It is there, but we won't hear it unless we listen for it.

'The Lord saith...'

Probably most charismatic churches have one or two people who regularly bring 'words from the Lord' to every service or meeting. Are these people special in some way? Do you think to yourself, 'How do *they* manage to hear God and I never hear anything? Are all these words really from God?'

Well, the answer to those questions is no. No, they are not special – you too can hear from God. And no, not every 'word' is a hundred per cent from God's mouth. It is our sinful, self-centred humanity that causes us either to say what we think the congregation ought to hear (though this may well be appropriate) or to add our own embellishments. Sometimes the message is ten per cent God and ninety per cent us – but that doesn't make God's ten per cent untrue or not worth saying. Those who hear these words have a responsibility to sort out the wheat from the chaff, and this is not just the responsibility of the minister or leader, but of every person in the congregation (1 Cor 14:29). The criteria for evaluating someone else's message is the same as before. Does it square with Scripture? Is it true? What do other, wiser Christians think?

Words from God which are given to us for the benefit of individuals or of groups of people such as a church or fellowship, and words which tell us something apt about someone else, are manifestations of the gifts of prophecy and knowledge. Words such as these must be used with care and probably do need to be checked first with the leadership: much harm can be done if they are passed on indiscriminately. If a message comes to you which you feel is for someone else, it won't 'go bad' while you check it out or pray about it before offering it in humility to those it is for.

We all struggle with prayer and find it difficult to see or hear answers to prayer. We do not always recognise the answer when it comes, because of our expectations either of the answer or of the way we think God will speak. When we think about answered or unanswered prayer, we usually think of our own prayers or those of people close to us with whom we have prayed, maybe for healing or for help out of a difficult situation. However, God may want us to *be* the answer to the prayers of others, even though we may not know them. This is when we need to hear God's prompting and act on it.

When I met Rita, I knew she was a 'fighter', but I didn't realise what a tough life she had had until she began to tell me how God had been so faithful. For five years she had been cramped in a poky flat in a problem-ridden high-rise development, struggling to keep moving on with God. She felt at the end of her tether physically, emotionally and spiritually. Few people realised this: Rita was not one to share her problems, even in prayer.

One desperate day, she threw up a short, succinct prayer to God: 'I could really do with a holiday, Lord.' No visions of sunny beaches or luxury hotels passed through her mind: only the knowledge that she needed restoring in body, mind and spirit.

A week later, Rita was completely amazed to get a letter from Lee Abbey in Devon (a Christian place of renewal, refreshment and restoration). An unknown person had paid for her to have a week's holiday there. She never found out who her benefactor was – she prays that God will bless them one hundredfold – and she never ceases to thank God for his answer to her prayer.

Now one way, now another

Over the years I have come to appreciate that while the chief way God speaks to us is through Scripture (and Scripture is the basis on which we evaluate all other means by which he communicates with us), God speaks to us in a number of ways. In the book of Job, Elihu tells Job that God speaks 'now one way, now another' (33:14).

God will speak to us in a way we can hear and to which we can respond because he speaks a universal language. He speaks to us through our ears, our eyes and our senses. He speaks to us through signs and symbols, through dreams and visions, through the Bible and through words that move us deeply. We don't have to be super-spiritual, very saintly or somehow have a special 'hot line' to heaven. We just have to love Jesus, be committed to him and yearn for a close relationship with him.

God will use different ways to speak to different people. Elijah heard him not in earthquake or fire, but in a gentle whisper (1 Kings 19:12). Jeremiah likened his voice to 'a hammer that breaks rock in pieces' (Jer 23:29). God warned Joseph in a dream to take Mary and the baby Jesus to Egypt (Matt 2:13). He spoke to David through the prophet Nathan regarding his sin with Bathsheba (2 Sam 12:1–14). Before Jesus came, God spoke to his people mainly through the prophets who then declared what he had told them – though occasionally, like Jeremiah, they were instructed to use 'visual aids' such as a ruined belt, a smashed clay pot or a yoke as symbols to reinforce God's message. However, he also spoke directly, for example to Joshua (Josh 1:1–9), Gideon (Judges 6,7), and Peter, James and John as they stood trembling on the mountain top while Jesus was transfigured before them: 'This is my Son, whom I love; with him

I am well pleased' he said. *'Listen* to him' (Matt 17:5, my italics).

In 1738, John Wesley's heart was 'strangely warmed' as he heard a sermon on part of Romans; he then went on with his brother, Charles, to initiate the great Evangelical Revival. Many great missionaries have heard God's voice in different ways, calling them to a particular part of the world. And ordinary people like you and me can hear him in our perfectly ordinary lives as we bring our prayers and praises to him.

Christians today not only have the words of the prophets and the other writers of what we know as the Old Testament to teach us; we also have the words and teaching of Jesus himself in the Gospels. We have the God-inspired letters of Paul and other disciples to guide us. God speaks to us as a church through these words, but he also speaks to us personally and intimately. God speaks to us through what we hear or what we feel; through pictures, visions and dreams; and he uses other people, his creation and other, more unusual visual aids. So why don't we always hear him?

Lazy learning?

'How can I hear God speaking to me?' 'How do I know it's *God* speaking and not my imagination?' These are two of the most frequently asked questions by Christians young and old. God wants us to hear his voice. Why do so many of us find it so hard to hear him?

Perhaps we in the western world are obsessed by information that comes instantly, overlaid with action. We expect television to show us events as they happen, and newspapers and books to give us 'the facts'. We are bombarded on all sides with words and images telling us to buy this, use that, live like this. We don't have to do much thinking at all. Pictures and 'facts' – whether right or wrong, good, bad or indifferent – are handed to us on a plate. Illustrations, jazzy visuals, computer graphics and virtual reality make it easy to pick up superficial information. 'Factional' documentaries on TV give us the impression we know all there is to know about a subject.

Sometimes when students get to college or university, they find it hard to order their personal study. They discover that many textbooks consist of pages and pages of close writing, with never an illustration to relieve the monotony! Learning as intelligent understanding and critical assimilation can be foreign soil to some. Many find it hard to adjust to this and experience depression and discouragement.

Do we expect God to make it easy for us? Do our prayers consist of questions that demand factual answers? Do we ask, 'Should I take this job/marry that person?' and expect a straight yes or no? Do we look for God's instructions to be picked out with flashing neon lights? Do we expect God to do our common-sense thinking for us? Do we gloss over the 'difficult' bits of the Bible and concentrate on the comforting promises?

God, being who he is – sovereign, almighty, all powerful, all knowing, loving, compassionate and concerned for us to grow to become Christlike – may indeed answer us with a direct yes or no. Or he may desire that we move on into spiritual maturity, leaving behind the primary school worksheet and going on to the adult reading.

God wants you to hear his voice. He encourages you to seek him in the world around you; to stop your questions and long prayers; to be silent; to hear that still, small voice he uses as he whispers to you. He wants you to open your eyes and ears to see and hear his voice in his creation. He may speak through preachers, teachers or the person sitting next to you. His conversation with you may be like that of a lover who speaks in sighs and looks, who needs no words – a sign or a light touch on the body conveys all the answer you need. Or he may just say, as he did to me that day, 'Read the Bible.'

You don't have to be a vicar, minister, pastor or elder to hear God's voice. You don't have to have a ministry of prophecy or healing or anything else. It doesn't matter if you are desperately juggling with the demands of home, children and a job, or struggling to maintain a family life with no money or partner. You simply have to open your ears and eyes, and be willing to listen for God's voice amid the noise, the din and the demands of the world around you.

Chapter 2

IS THIS REALLY YOU, LORD?

I had a friend once who, when she phoned me, would always announce, 'Hello! It's me!' Unfortunately, her voice was very like that of another friend of mine, and I have a very slight hearing defect which is aggravated when using the phone; so I was never very sure who was calling me. I didn't have the sense (or courage) to tell her this, so I used to struggle with the conversation for the first half-minute or so until I cottoned on to who she was!

It can be like that with God. If only he would announce clearly, 'This is God speaking!' But God is more than just a friend: he is our heavenly Father and we are his children. Children quickly learn their parents' voices because they have plenty of practice at listening to them. God wants us to be familiar with his voice, but if only we would practice listening to him! The more we listen for his voice, the more we will hear it, not just with our ears but with our whole being. And the more we hear it, the more familiar it will become. When her baby cries, any first-time mother worries that something is wrong and spends the first week of her baby's life rushing upstairs to check that all is well. After that she rapidly becomes familiar with her baby's voice and can pick it out in a crowd. On a Sunday morning in church, I see the young mothers occasionally cock an ear towards the door of the crèche, and it's always the right one who goes out to give a cuddle and some reassurance. (OK, sometimes a father will go out, but usually he has to be nudged!) Learning to hear God's voice is a little bit like that.

Sometimes we think God has spoken to us, but we are not too sure that it is him and not just wishful thinking or a vivid imagination. How can we check this out?

Is it biblical?
First and foremost, we need to determine whether what we have heard is biblical. Does it agree with Scripture?

If you receive a word or instruction which does not conform with what is written in the Bible, then it is *not* God speaking. The Bible is the word of God. We have in the Bible what he has said and how others have heard him, right through from Genesis to Revelation. He will never contradict himself. So, for example, if we think that God is telling us it is OK to go and live with someone who is already married, however pure, wonderful and 'predestined' we may feel our love is for that person, then we are not hearing God. He takes sin very seriously (Deut 5:18).

Janet was in a desperately unhappy marriage. She had become a Christian fairly late in life, and now their two sons had grown up and left home. She wondered how she could cope any longer. Her husband

Keith subjected her to emotional blackmail, continually belittling her. Her new-found faith only seemed to add fuel to the flames of his unkindness.

Janet confided in Audrey, a friend she had made at church. Audrey was a woman her own age, who had had a similarly unhappy marriage which had ended in divorce. Audrey advised Janet to confront Keith: 'Refuse to do things for him. Show him you are not going to be treated like dirt. Tell him how you feel.'

Janet listened carefully. After all, Audrey was a much more mature Christian than she was. She herself wasn't too sure about confronting Keith and didn't think it would result in anything but another row. However, she thought that she would try to tell him how she felt and maybe even give as good as she got. A bit of his own medicine wouldn't do any harm. Janet found that her actions only made things worse.

Feeling desperate, she began to read her Bible more carefully. As she did, she came to realise that God's instructions are not conditional upon another person's behaviour. The fruit that God wants to grow in our lives – love, joy, peace, patience, kindness, goodness, faithfulness, gentleness and self-control – does not depend on that fruit first growing in others (Gal 5:22–26). God will never tell us to do something contrary to his principles of mercy, justice and righteousness. He requires that we love others as we love ourselves (Matt 22:39) and forgive others as he has forgiven us (6:12–14). He will never tell us that it is right to 'pay someone back' for what they have done, however attractive the idea may seem (Lev 19:18). Tit-for-tat is not the Christian way.

When Janet stopped asking God to change Keith and concentrated instead on becoming the person God wanted her to be, she began to see a transformation in her relationship with Keith.

What does the Bible say?

Of course, to check out what we think God is saying to us, we need to know what the Bible says. Research shows that there has been a big drop, over the last ten years or so, in the number of Christians who read the Bible. One of the reasons is undoubtedly the pressure of day-to-day living, but there is another, more subtle factor. In society today there is a great emphasis on experience, on what we feel. Truth is relative: 'if something is right for you, it is not necessarily right for me'. This has spilled over into the church, and many Christians are more concerned with experiencing blessings than with basing those blessings on God's word and God's truth. There seems to be a 'pick-and-mix' attitude towards faith – 'I like this bit, but not that' – and the 'difficult' bits of the Bible are shrugged off as 'cultural anomalies' that don't apply to us. Bible study has moved into the technological age, with dozens of electronic Scripture aids, guides round the Holy Land and interactive Bible games. Everything is made easy to use and consumer-friendly. Even some Bible reading notes seem more like a 'thought for the day', with a short verse and a quick comment passing itself off as 'Bible reading'. The danger is that reading the Bible becomes superficial, the games and electronic aids easy to turn off.

When my husband got a new software program for

his computer, he fiddled about with this bit and that bit, and tried to do what he wanted the program to do. Eventually, he had to turn to the Tutorial and Help pages and learn how to do the thing properly. We need to be equally clear about biblical basics. There is no substitute for regular Bible reading, aided by thoughtful and challenging notes.

I can't do that!

Sometimes it seems that what God is telling us to do is against all our natural inclinations. Although in our hearts we may acknowledge the biblical rightness of what he is asking us to do, it seems impossible, and we think it can't really be God saying this.

During World War II, Corrie Ten Boom was imprisoned in Ravensbruck, the notorious Nazi prison where thousands of women were brutalised, tortured and killed. Corrie's sister, Betsie, died in that dreadful prison, as did countless others. Two years after the end of the war, Corrie came face to face with one of the prison's most cruel guards, who had since become a Christian. She was paralysed with horror. He wanted her forgiveness, but she felt that this was impossible: the memory of his cruelty was still fresh in her mind. Yet she knew that God's message of forgiveness is conditional upon our forgiveness of those who have injured us. To receive God's forgiveness, her own heart had to be forgiving. By calling upon Jesus, she found it possible to forgive and love the former guard.

Have you prayed about it?

Has God spoken to you in response to your prayers? As well as being scriptural, is what you have heard relevant? God does answer prayer, but not always in the way we expect.

When my husband retired, we moved from the south of England up to Cheshire to be nearer our family. Although I was delighted that I would be nearer my daughter and grandsons, I was rather fearful I would not find so loving and supportive a church as the one I'd been attending since I became a Christian.

For a large part of my married life I have suffered from repeated bouts of clinical depression, and still do battle with it even now. When I became a Christian, I found things very hard. At that time our marriage was not very good and, with my changed life focus, my husband and I had less in common. The fact that he worked irregular hours meant it was difficult to find a regular daily time to be alone with God. I quickly discovered that the best times to pray were when I took the dog for his early morning walk in the local woods, which probably explains why God speaks to me so much through the natural world around me. So I was concerned over our move and asked God many times to lead me to the right church. After much prayer, I felt God say to me, 'I will not leave you an orphan' (John 14:18).

For over three years, I went to four or five churches of different denominations and asked God many times, 'Is this the right church?' Struggling with a new home, few friends and my newly-retired, non-Christian husband, I would have been very grateful if God had just said, 'Go to church A.' But all I got was, 'I will not leave you an orphan.' It was not until I joined my present fellowship that I realised what he had been saying all along, that orphans have no family and that he was going to put me in a real Christian family. Had I gone there straightaway, I would not have appreciated the depth of God's love, his concern that I should understand the profundity of what he was saying, and the wonderful love and care of that fellowship for me. All I would have noticed, perhaps, were the superficial differences from what I had been used to. I thank God deeply now for that time of depression and unhappiness, though I admit to shouting at him more than once at the time!

Are you obedient?

When God answers our prayers, even though it is not always what we expect or want, it is vital that we still thank him and that we are obedient. Obedience is a necessary component, a vital part, of our walk with God. Ingratitude and disobedience can block our ears and hearts to God's words.

In his story about the two men who built houses (Matt 7:24–27), Jesus likened the man who built on sand to those who heard God's word but did not obey it; while the man who built on rock was like those who heard his word and put it into practice. The two houses looked alike and both stood firmly – until the storm and rains came, and disaster overtook the sand-based house.

On the unstable coast of East Suffolk, most of Dunwich village has disappeared into the sea as the waves have eaten into the loose soil of the cliffs. Over the years, houses, shops, churches have all vanished beneath the waters. Each stormy high tide nibbles away at the remaining soil. I often think of Dunwich when I read those words of Jesus. Those houses looked firm and solid, but now they are gone. Our lives, our Christian lives, may look firmly based, but unless they are based on obedience to what God commands, then adversity will bring destruction.

In John 15, Jesus used the analogy of a vine to tell us to 'remain in' him; and to remain in his love, we must obey his command to love one another as he loved us – to the point of death. All vine growers know that to produce worthwhile fruit, the vines have to be pruned and trained. It is no good letting a vine rampage everywhere! Pruning involves cutting back healthy-looking branches almost nearly to their base, so that the energy of the vine is directed towards producing fruit. The prunings will not bear fruit; only the part that remains attached to the vine will. This is how we must be, pruned by God and remaining faithful to his commands. God's promises require our obedience.

In 1853, James Hudson Taylor obeyed God's call to take the gospel into China, that great and mysterious country which had been isolated from the rest of the world for so long. He ignored most of the conventions of his day and endeavoured to identify with the Chinese people, dressing in Chinese clothing and expecting his students to follow his example.

When William Wilberforce campaigned against the slave trade, he incurred the wrath of many wealthy businessmen whose status and livelihood depended on the continuance of slavery. Wilberforce's position in Parliament, to which he was certain God had called him, enabled him to have influence among those with the power to stop the trade. Despite years of frustration and disappointment, he continued his campaign in obedience to what God had called him to do.

Ananias (Acts 9) was obviously a godly man: when God called his name, his immediate response was, 'Yes, Lord.' But he was given instructions that he would probably rather not have heard – to go to Saul, that terrible persecutor of believers in Jesus, and actually lay his hands on him to restore his sight! 'You are joking, aren't you, Lord?' But Ananias was obedient and trusted God for his own safety. He sought Saul out and laid his hands on his head. Immediately, Saul's sight was restored; he was baptised and became Paul, the great apostle to the Gentiles. We don't hear any more in the Bible about Ananias, but I am sure the Lord kept speaking to him. His ears and heart were completely open to God's voice, and his obedience contributed to the spread of the gospel.

Did I hear this right?

It is quite in order for us to ask God if we have heard him, or heard him correctly as Ananias did. We can say something like, 'Lord, I believe you are saying I should do this/go there/speak to that person. I want to make sure that I am hearing you and not my own voice. Please confirm your words to me.' If this is God speaking to you, then you will find confirmation – but you have to be listening! It may be that you are drawn to a particular verse in the Bible which will shout out, 'Yes!' It may be you hear a sermon or word in church which seems directed straight towards you, or you may feel a great sense of peace over the matter.

A few years ago, at a special meeting of our local home groups, I felt the Holy Spirit pushing me strongly to speak, although the relevance of what I was to say to the gathering seemed minimal, to say the least! However, the urge became strong, and I eventually got up and said what I felt God was wanting me to say. As I feared, it went down like a lead balloon. The elder leading the service said kindly that perhaps we needed to think about that word. However, after the meeting, as we were chatting over coffee, a man I knew only slightly came up and said, 'That word was for me. It was the answer to a problem I have been praying about for some time. Thank you.' I was very humbled to think that God had used me – who was nearly too nervous to speak out – as the confirmation this man needed. (I think he was a bit surprised, too!)

It may be that you will not hear confirmation. Events will just 'fall into place'; the right person 'by chance' is in the right place at the right time. Co-incidences are often God-incidences. The apostle Peter received a vision from God which he felt was contrary to God's laws on clean and unclean food (Acts 11:1–18), so he argued with God. But God persisted and, although Peter was still wondering about the meaning of his vision, events quickly confirmed what the Lord was saying to Peter, with the result that the gospel spread among the Gentiles.

Have you checked it out?

Everyone needs a wise, mature Christian friend. Even wise, mature Christians need wise and mature friends, especially if they are in a leadership position. We need friends whose wisdom and discretion we can rely on, with whom we can talk and pray about what we feel God is saying to us. Very often in talking it over we will get a sense of the rightness or otherwise of what we feel God might be asking us to do. It is easy to get carried away with a scheme which is intrinsically godly and for which we feel great enthusiasm, but which is not God's plan *for us*. We may need the humility to accept it when someone says, 'Do you think this is quite right for you? Wouldn't it be better if so-and-so took it on?'

Following the disintegration of Communism and the overthrow of President Ceausescu, my local church sent a team over to Romania with medicines, provisions, seeds, etc, together with Bibles and Christian literature. They needed volunteers for a second and third trip, to follow up their contacts and take other much-needed Christian literature. Fired up by this I decided to volunteer, despite the misgivings of my husband who, because of his irregular working hours, felt that he needed someone at home. I was able to get time off from work and told everyone what I was doing, enjoying their astonished admiration. I attended all the meetings, convinced that God was in all this. After several frustrating delays, which no one seemed able to explain, the leader of the group gently said to me, 'Do you really think you are the right person for this venture?' I was deeply hurt and very upset, but I had to admit he was right. It wouldn't have been the right thing for me to do at that time and, if I am honest, I envisaged much of the glory going to me, not to God.

King David, despite his failings, was 'a man after God's heart'. He longed to build a great temple for the glory of God. But, through the prophet Nathan, God told David that it would be his son Solomon who would build the temple (1 Chron 22). David, whose leadership had welded the Israelites into a powerful, and godly nation, would not be able to crown his reign in this way. Instead, his son was to have that honour.

Is God not saying anything, or is it me?

If you are a parent, or have anything to do with young (and not-so-young) children, you will know that at times you can talk to them until you are blue in the face, but it makes not the slightest difference. They are not deaf – they can hear the bells of an ice-cream van from miles away. It's just that their absorption in their own activities is blocking your words out. I reckon our heavenly Father must feel very like an earthly parent sometimes. He is calling us, but we are so self-absorbed we don't hear a thing!

What particular things can block your ears? Are you talking so much, you can't hear him? Some prayer meetings I've been to never give the Lord a chance to reply. We must never forget that prayer is a two-way conversation. Many people seem afraid of silence and rush to fill it up with more prayer, or praise and thanksgiving.

Does silence make you feel uncomfortable? Can you think of a reason why? Sometimes it has to do with the sort of person you are. Some like to recharge their inner batteries by being with other people: they feel alive and reinvigorated in company, and hate being on their own. Others feel the need for solitude to refresh themselves and get back on an even keel: they find the constant company of others draining. There is no right or wrong attitude; we each respond according to the temperament God has given us. Obviously, it is easier for those who enjoy solitude to quieten themselves and wait in silence for God's presence to become apparent. However, we do all need to give God time to speak to us.

I'm sure you have friends who greet you, 'How are you?', then don't stop talking until they finish, 'Must rush! Lovely to chat!'

'Who's chatting?' you think. 'I couldn't get a word in edgeways…'

Noise seems to be a constant companion these days: radios are on all the time; personal stereos are clamped to ears; in-car music accompanies every journey; mobile phones keep ringing. There seems hardly a minute when noise from outside is not being fed into our heads. We need to give God a chance to get through, to quieten our minds and focus on him.

'Be still, and know that I am God' (Psalm 46:10). There is a place for silence when words are inappropriate. You may find it easier to remain still if you think about God himself – his love, faithfulness, compassion, might and power; or you can say, very quietly to yourself, an appropriate verse or verses from one of the psalms. Finding time to be silent can be almost impossible for some harassed souls, but God knows this. If you are willing to listen in even the tiniest time-slot, he will speak. You will hear his voice cutting through the clamour and hubbub, straight to your heart.

Are our minds too full of trivia?

'Every time I try to think about God, all sorts of silly things come into my head.'

Is this you? It certainly is me, and I suspect it applies to a great many Christians. If we could see what everyone was thinking during a Sunday morning service, I wonder what we'd find. An awful lot about the Sunday dinner, probably, and the usual worries: 'Are the children behaving themselves?' 'Does he/she really like me?' 'How will I get through that meeting tomorrow?' These thoughts are not wrong in themselves: we all have thoughts. It's what we do with them that matters. The psalmist prayed, 'May the words of my mouth and the meditation of my heart be pleasing in your sight, O Lord, my Rock and my Redeemer' (Psalm 19:14).

Meditation is what you do when you take hold of a thought and chew it over, thinking about the subject until the whole of your mind is occupied with it. Meditation on God's word from the Bible is good, for then the whole of your mind is given over to God. But intrusive thoughts that enter while you are trying to concentrate on God don't need to be given priority. Try dismissing them, 'Not now', and pushing them out of your mind, perhaps by saying a verse like 'My lips will praise you' or 'Lord, you are my Rock and my Redeemer'. If the thought that has intruded is one you want to remember later, then quickly jot it down on a small notepad, firmly put it away and return to God.

Our minds these days can be filled to overflowing with other matters. Some of these are important (our families or our work), and some are trivial (TV 'soaps', gossip, the latest media sensation). The outcry that occurs when a 'soap' character is killed, dies or jailed makes me wonder if many people can separate real life from fiction!

Genuine worries and concerns can be placed before God. 'Cast all your anxiety on him because he cares for you' (1 Pet 5:7). If you have really deep concerns, it is not always easy to do this. If this is the case, you may find it helpful to imagine yourself leading the person or people you are worried about by the hand to Jesus, and putting their hands in his. Alternatively, you could just tell Jesus the names of those who concern you and ask him to look after them; or write their names on a piece of paper, put it in an envelope and place it somewhere away from you, telling God that you have given them to him. Whatever you do, it is real and true that God will shoulder your burdens; then your mind and attention can be wholly given to him.

Trivial matters must be seen for what they are – unimportant. As we learn more about God, his creative might and power, and his enormous, unending love and compassion for us, we will be able to get the right perspective on life. 'Be concerned above everything else with the Kingdom of God and with what he requires of you' (Matt 6:33, GNB).

If our minds are continually filled with non-important matters, then we are not available for God. Too often we regard our 'time with God' as a slot early in the morning or last thing at night, which we carve out of our time almost as a favour to him, or as a duty to be done and dusted so that we can get on with the rest of our lives. We 'make time for God', not realising that our time, our whole lives, are his and we are totally in his hands. We need to be listening, we need to be available for what God wants, and we need humility to take on board what he is saying and how he is saying it. God cannot use proud, arrogant people, and it is an inherent sin of humankind that we want to do things our own way. The psalmist tell us, 'Though the Lord is on high, he looks upon the lowly, but the proud he knows from afar' (Psalm 138:6). God has an intimate relationship with the lowly and the humble. He looks upon them with favour. But the proud and arrogant he keeps at a distance: they will never see his face nor hear his voice in that close relationship with him we all crave. Confession is a good start to our conversation with God.

Listening to God is an exciting, challenging and awesome experience. It is a little bit like learning another language. We need to attune our inner ears to different words, sounds and inflexions. Above all we need to keep practising.

Chapter 3

A WORD FOR ME?

The congregation settled down as Steve, our pastor, picked up the microphone and opened his Bible. What, we wondered, was Steve going to come up with this morning? Our meetings were never bland, ordinary or the same each week, and he usually managed to challenge us in some way.

'How many of you have heard from God this week?' he asked.

A couple of somewhat tentative hands were raised amid some rather wary faces. What was he after?

'How many of you have read the Bible this week?' he went on.

A great many more confident hands were raised. We felt on surer ground here!

'Then you have heard from God.'

Steve shut his Bible with a bang and, wearing a big grin, waved it in the air. 'This is God's word to us, now, this week. If you've read what he is saying, you've heard from God.'

The Bible is God speaking to us

Steve was illustrating a profound truth. If someone asked you, 'Have you heard from so-and-so lately?', you might reply, 'Yes, I got a letter from him last week.' Because you received a written communication, you feel that you have 'heard' from that person – how he is and what his plans are – in exactly the same way as you might have heard him speak.

Sometimes, though, letters are not very personal. I get a lot of junk mail (don't we all!) which starts, 'Dear Mrs Peall…' and then urges me to buy or join something, or send money to save something. But I know that hundreds of others have received a 'personal' letter like that: it isn't really personal to me.

Reading the Bible can feel a bit like that (impersonal, not junk mail!). We can study it, analyse it, even treat it all in a very special, reverent way. Hundreds of books and commentaries on various parts of the Bible have been published, and Bible study groups abound. In some churches, the Bible is treated almost as an object of worship itself, particularly in the Orthodox traditions. On holiday in Greece I was amazed to see a beautiful, ornate Bible on a carved lectern in the centre of the church being reverently kissed by the many Greeks as they came in. Thinking about it afterwards, I wondered if some traditions in the UK have gone too far in the opposite direction, treating the Bible as an 'add-on' extra to what we feel and experience.

Jesus said to the Pharisees, 'You diligently study the Scriptures because you think that by them you possess eternal life. These are the Scriptures that testify about me, yet you refuse to come to me to have life' (John 5:39–40). We too can diligently study God's word, yet refuse to make a commitment to Jesus; we can worship the Bible, yet refuse to worship its author.

One member of our home group, who had been brought up in a church-going family, described how boring and dry he had found the Bible before he became, as he put it, a 'real' Christian. Then, he said, it was like a light being switched on. He couldn't get enough of it, even though he didn't always understand it. From being a 'diligent searcher', he had become one who had received life. The Bible had come alive for him.

Steve was right to say that when we read the Bible, we are hearing from God. We don't have to be especially intelligent, trained or in any particular position of authority. The Bible is not a set of stories from which we can gather a few truths: it *is* truth. It tells us about God, his character, his plans and his purposes for his people and his church. However, Steve didn't tell us the whole story (and I know he would agree). He wanted to make a point and to challenge us – and he did! But before we get a personal letter, we need to have established a relationship with its sender. My junk mail may begin, 'Dear Mrs Peall', but it is not personal because I do not have any sort of relationship with the firm or organisation that sent it. The letters I like are the ones that begin, 'My dear Gillian...'

Will God speak to me, personally?

'I've made a commitment to Jesus,' you may be saying. 'Why then do I never feel God has spoken to me personally?'

A good question. If your thoughts are running along these lines, you may be doubting the integrity of your faith. Let me reassure you. However dry you feel, however much you feel that God does not speak to you, if you have given your heart and life to Jesus, then *you belong to God*. 'You will seek me and find me when you seek me with all your heart,' God told the people of Israel through the prophet Jeremiah (Jer 29:13). If you are really seeking to hear God, you will hear his voice.

But – and it is a very big but – we must never read the Bible as though it was *only* a personal word for us. When we do, we tend to ignore the bits we don't think apply to us. Our thinking becomes distorted, which in turn can lead to heresy. Everything in the Bible is there to guide, comfort and teach us. As well as speaking to us personally, the Bible has another, equally important function, which is to act as the measure against which all our other experiences and 'words from God' must be judged. This cannot be stressed too strongly. Because a Christian has had a certain experience, this does not mean that it was a *Christian* experience and therefore the norm for all other Christians. A picture or dream may well be the way God chooses to speak to some, but it may not be the way God chooses to speak to others: the pictures and dreams they experience may not be from God. Everything must be judged against what the Bible has to say. Some parts of the Bible may seem obscure or confusing, but the basics are usually very clear. Gordon Fee and Douglas Stuart, in their excellent book *How to Read the Bible for all its Worth*, say,

'The single most serious problem people have with the Bible is not with a lack of understanding, but with the fact that they understand most things too well!'

Paul told Timothy, his young fellow disciple, that 'All Scripture is God-breathed and is useful for teaching, rebuking, correcting and training in righteousness (2 Tim 3:16). Note the bit about rebuking and correcting: not all Scripture is there just to bring us comfort and encouragement when we are feeling fragile. It is there to train us to be men and women of God. We may well find that a passage of Scripture makes us feel uncomfortable or challenged, or points us to the need for repentance.

Is it wrong, then, to have favourite verses? No, of course not. Very often when we have found that a verse has helped us in the past, we can recall it, knowing it will help us again. It is useful to note these verses down so that we can refer to them quickly in times of trouble, when we need encouragement or to remind ourselves just who we are in Christ. However, we must guard against searching Scripture *for the answers we want*. So many of the comforting 'promises' that are trotted out so glibly have conditional clauses attached to them.

Cast your cares on him

However committed we are to Jesus, it is still very easy to read the Bible and not feel that it is relevant to you. You may feel you have never had a personal word from God, or you may have in the past but are feeling that God has 'shut up shop' and gone away. If this is your experience, then you are not alone.

Probably all of us at some time have felt distant from both God and his word. We may understand what all the verses mean, but it doesn't seem to get through to that part of us which is feeling desperately dry, worried sick, depressed, stressed out.

Knowing your way round the Bible will help, so that when you are feeling like this you can readily turn to a verse that will speak to your particular circumstances. You can take the verse, or passage, make it personal and speak it back to God.

> How long, O Lord? Will you forget me for ever?
>   How long will you hide your face from me?
> How long must I wrestle with my thoughts
>   and every day have sorrow in my heart?
> How long will my enemy triumph over me?
>
> *(Psalm 13:1–2)*

I have read the verses of this psalm, spoken them out loud to God, whenever I've been badly depressed. Depression is my enemy: yours might be worry, persecution, fear, or anything else that is keeping you from God. But, like the psalmist, we have to acknowledge the sovereignty and goodness of God, however we feel. We have to declare, as a statement of our commitment:

> But I trust in your unfailing love;
>   my heart rejoices in your salvation.
> I will sing to the Lord
>   for he has been good to me.
>
> *(Psalm 13:5–6)*

Some years ago I was trying to make a decision about something I really wanted to do. It would have involved making a long-term commitment on a regular basis, and I wasn't sure that this was going to be possible or right. My own home circumstances were not easy, and I could see that my mother and my mother-in-law would need help from me in the near future.

Now I am the sort of person who likes to get decisions made and everything settled quickly. Uncertainty makes me uncomfortable. I can imagine that half of you are nodding your heads in sympathetic agreement, and the other half are thinking, 'How awful to have to make your mind up in such a rush!' But that's the way we are.

At the time I was reading Jeremiah, and one verse really jumped out at me:

'Stand at the crossroads and look;
    ask for the ancient paths,
ask where the good way is, and walk in it,
    and you will find rest for your souls.'

(Jeremiah 6:16)

I was stunned. Here was God telling me quite clearly to wait, not to rush into a decision and, not only that, to ask for advice as to the godly course of action. Me – who prided myself on being a quick decision-maker! I did wait, and I did take wise counsel, and I didn't do what I wanted to do. As it turned out, it was a jolly good thing I didn't. That verse has helped me several times since, in all sorts of circumstances.

If you have found that a particular verse 'jumps out' at you from the passage you are reading, then perhaps God is speaking to you. If it seems to have neon lights around it, then he is. For me, the Jeremiah verse not only had neon lights, it seemed to have bells too! But don't be tempted to take a verse out of context. The verses around it may be equally important and may well qualify the promises made. Jesus spoke of God the Father forgiving our sins – but it is necessary both to repent of those sins *and* to forgive others (Matt 6:12). We know that God loves us – but we are commanded to *love one another as he loves us* (John 15:12).

God may also choose to bring a passage to your attention time and time again, within a short space of time. Wendy found that God chased her around with Scriptures – but I will let her tell her own story:

> Roger Jones and a team from Christian Music Ministries had visited my church in 1994 and 1996, and CMM was invited to visit the church in 1998. The plan was to produce the latest musical by Roger Jones, called *Pharisee*, based around Nicodemus who, Jesus says, 'must be born again' (see John's Gospel). An inter-church choir would be formed for the event, plus the CMM cast and soloists.
>
> The theme song uses the words from Luke 4:18: 'The Spirit of the Lord is upon me…' Another song is 'Dry Bones', referring to the valley of dry bones in Ezekiel 37. And my favourite talks of 'streams of living water flowing from your heart'.

In 1997, after a few very difficult months, things in general went pear-shaped and it looked as if the *Pharisee* visit would have to be cancelled. At church one Sunday morning, I was talking to God about the musical while trying to keep half an ear open to the visiting preacher who was delivering her sermon. In desperation I said to God, 'Lord, I just can't do it!' At that moment the preacher said, 'You go forward not in your own strength, but in the Lord's anointing.' I sat up at that! Was this from God, or just a coincidence? I felt I probably had the answer a few minutes later when she started to talk about Nicodemus the Pharisee and what Jesus said to him: 'You must be born again'.

She had no idea of the turmoil I was in.

A couple of weeks later I went to the evening service, where there was another visiting preacher who knew nothing about the *Pharisee* project. He preached on the text, 'The Spirit of the Lord is upon me'. Another coincidence?

Shortly after this I reached the point where I desperately needed some space and time to think and pray through a situation I was facing, as well as to come to some sort of decision regarding the *Pharisee* production. To do this, I booked myself a month's 'holiday' from my home church and decided to go visiting. *(Wendy was the deacon in charge of worship at the time.)*

A couple of weeks later I visited a church where I was not known and settled down to enjoy the service. The pastor there, who I didn't know, spoke right into my situation. Not once, but all through! I was pinned to my chair! At the end of the service I could hardly believe it when the pastor offered to pray for all those who felt dry, dusty and worn out, that 'those rivers of living waters would flow out from your hearts'.

That evening I visited another church in the same group, another preacher, different message and yet more 'coincidences', both in the worship and the sermon, even in the conversations afterwards. God spoke to me in such a way through these people that it's still hard to believe. I kept a detailed journal to remind myself when it all got too unbelievable and, well, it reads like a novel!'

God continued to speak to Wendy through those Bible verses, through a prayer meeting, through her Bible reading notes and through a 'word' from someone she had never met before. As she says, 'I finally got the message!' The production of *Pharisee* was a huge success and many people heard God speak to them through it.

God spoke to Wendy through Scripture over a remarkably short period. However, his faithfulness can cover many years, as my friend Rita discovered long before she went to Lee Abbey. Rita had received an industrial injury when she was in the catering business and had to chase for compensation through the courts over a period of seven years. During the first four years she was in constant pain, but during that time had a powerful sense of God's love with her. Every time she was dealt a blow by the opposing side, God worked for her good and turned things around. He told Rita that he would make her righteousness shine like the dawn and the justice of her cause like the noonday sun (Psalm 37:6). She persevered, and God showed her that the opposing side were like Pharaoh in the book of Exodus, whose heart was hardened time and time again. Her opponents even resorted to videoing her secretly, to see if she was truly disabled by pain. She was shattered by this revelation and felt personally violated. But she turned to her Bible, to 2 Chronicles chapter 20. As she read verses 15–17, it was as if God was in the room with her: 'Do not be afraid of this vast army, for the battle is not yours but God's … You will not have to fight this battle. Take up your position, stand firm, and see the deliverance of the Lord'. Eventually the opposition was worn down, and they paid up. But Rita is convinced that God enabled her to have the victory, while the glory went to him.

It doesn't seem to mean anything to *me*!

'I read the Bible but nothing happens!'

This seems to be the case for most of us most of the time. Individual verses do not jump out at us every day, and while a verse a day is OK, more is definitely better. We really need to read the Bible regularly and in sizeable chunks, if possible.

If you are having difficulties in making Scripture personal to yourself, one thing that may help is to imagine God is speaking to you. I had great difficulty with this at first: when I read a passage I'd be thinking, 'It's all very well, but this is Paul writing to the Ephesians about Ephesian affairs; not God writing to me.' Well, yes it is. But Paul was inspired by God, and the Ephesians (or Romans or Corinthians or whoever) were people just like us. Many of us can read great poetry and share in the poet's emotions, identifying with him or her, even though we are not experiencing the same events. We can read the problem pages in a magazine and find answers there that can help us with our own problems. In the same way but with much greater effect, all Scripture can transcend the immediate events the writers may be referring to, and speak in a universal language across time and space.

If you are feeling lonely and far away from God, then Leviticus is not the place to go – but Psalm 13 might well help. The psalms are a good place to start. They were written from the heart by ordinary people like you and me, who suffered pain, persecution, sicknesses, and who felt dry, far from God and on the brink of despair. They were also written by those bubbling over with joy, thankfulness and praise for our great God. Imagine that you have written a psalm, then say it back to God. Reading it out loud helps enormously. Read it aloud every day until it becomes your own. Think about each verse as you read it. Is it beginning to mean something special to you?

Perhaps you are wondering if God is really there:

try Psalm 73. If you are feeling strong and confident, choose one of the praise psalms such as 93 or 95. Browse through the psalm, making the verses that seem to fit your circumstances personal, thinking of your situation as you say the psalm to God.

Alternatively, you could take Paul's beautiful prayer in Ephesians 3:14–21 and make it your own.

> Father, I kneel before you as part of the family of God. I pray that out of your glorious riches you will strengthen me with power through your Spirit in my inner being, so that Christ may dwell in my heart through faith. I pray that I, being rooted and established in love, may have power, together with all my brothers and sisters in Christ, to grasp how wide and long and high and deep is the love of Christ, and to know this love that surpasses knowledge – so that I may be filled to the measure of all the fullness of God. And I ask, Father, that I may hear your voice in my head and in my heart, that I may learn more and more of you and your love for me. Amen.

Whatever you do, do it with the expectancy that God will speak to you through his word. You will find that he will do just that. I promise you.

Chapter 4

IN THE MIND'S EYE

We all have imaginations. Without imagination there would be no creative art, no music, no literature; there would be no science, no inventions. No one would ever look at something and think, 'What if...?'

God has given us our imaginations; they are part of our God-given temperament and emotional make-up.

When they are praying or worshipping God, or listening to his word, many Christians see 'pictures' in their minds. Are these pictures 'just imagination' – or are they really, as many claim, given to them by God? Well, it all depends (although I know that answer sounds rather like a cop-out). God may well stir up the imagination so that we see in our minds something that will illuminate his words, or the words of others, and gain a deeper understanding of what he is saying. He used pictures to communicate with the prophets:

> The word of the Lord came to me: 'What do
> you see, Jeremiah?'
>   'I see the branch of an almond tree,' I
> replied.
>   The Lord said to me, 'You have seen

correctly, for I am watching to see that my
word is fulfilled.'

(Jeremiah 1:11–12)

And the Lord asked me, 'What do you see,
Amos?'
   'A plumb-line,' I replied.
   Then the Lord said, 'Look, I am setting a
plumb-line among my people Israel; I will
spare them no longer.'

(Amos 7:8)

A book that is solid text, with few or no illustrations,
is heavy going, as any student will testify! When you
are studying unfamiliar material, it is a great help to
have diagrams and drawings to help you understand
and to fix the topic in your mind. A gripping novel,
however, does not usually need illustrations: the
words themselves stimulate the imagination and give
the mind plenty to feed on in the way of images. My
mother, who was a great reader, used to get very
cross with TV adaptations of her favourite books.
'They've got it all wrong,' she would shout at the
screen. 'So-and-so never looked like that! She was
much prettier/shorter/darker or fairer!'

Every picture tells a story
Jesus knew how much the human mind needs pictures to accompany words, so he spoke in parables –
picture stories – to give his teaching more impact.
The Jews knew religious instruction as a set of

minute rules and regulations, and Jesus' radical new teaching needed to engage their hearts and imaginations to take them out of the old mind-set.

Jesus didn't only use parables: he used vivid metaphors and figures of speech to imprint what he was saying on the minds of his listeners. Stories of sheep and goats, an unmerciful servant, the wise and foolish virgins, the prodigal son, all had a deep spiritual meaning behind the obvious story-line. It was up to his listeners to sort out the meaning and relate it to their own lives (although sometimes the disciples still felt they were in the dark and had to ask Jesus to explain something).

Jesus seasoned his speech with word-pictures. He spoke of his disciples being 'fishers of men' (Matt 4:19) – and he didn't mean they were literally going to throw their nets into the Sea of Galilee and catch bodies! He told them that they were the salt of the earth, lights to the world (Matt 5:13–14). He talked about wedding feasts, patches on garments and old wine bottles made of skin. He likened himself to a mother hen with her chicks under her wings (Luke 13:34). He used everyday examples, things and events that would be familiar to his listeners, to bring home his teachings. Language such as this is vivid, colourful and sets the imagination working, bringing pictures to the mind, illustrating God's word from personal experience and thus rooting it firmly in the heart. And Jesus' listeners had to listen. They didn't have the written Gospels, as we do, to pore over, examine and analyse. They couldn't read all about it in the newspapers the next day. What Jesus said had to get through, or be lost. It had to make an impact first time round. Today his words retain the immediacy, clarity and impact they had two thousand years ago.

We too need to hear God's word and relate it to our own lives by picturing it in our minds. And this is not 'just our imagination'; rather, our minds are working as God intended, bringing alive his word in our lives. When they are speaking on a particular Bible passage, many preachers and teachers will start off by 'setting the scene'. For example, for the wedding of Cana, we hear how huge the water jars were, or what sort of ceremonies and celebrations went on at a Jewish wedding in the first century AD. And we try to imagine how miraculous it all seemed. But reading the passage to ourselves may result in a more fertile picture if we will allow our minds and our imaginations to help us.

Why not picture a wedding you have been involved in, maybe your own, or your son's or daughter's, or even that of a close friend? Feel the humiliation when the caterers discover there isn't enough wine for everyone to toast the bride. Imagine Jesus there, telling the catering staff to fill up the empties from the tap and take them into the reception. Sounds crazy that way, doesn't it? How would the caterers or the restaurant staff feel as they held the bottles under the taps, then wrapped them in white napkins or put them in ice buckets? And out comes vintage champagne, far better than the cheap sparkling white wine that had originally been available.

Using your God-given imagination in this way can

really help you to grasp the truth of Jesus' teaching and apply it in your own life.

Pictures given by God

Sometimes pictures seem to come from nowhere and appear to have little relevance to the matter in hand. They seem to enter our minds when we are especially open to God, perhaps when we are worshipping or praying. When they come, they can be particularly valuable, enhancing our worship or telling us how we are to pray more precisely into a problem.

Pictures that come while you are praying should be examined for a while. Are they for you alone, so that your prayers can be more focused? If you are praying with one other person, or in a group, should the pictures be shared? I have a friend who is very gifted by God in the way she receives pictures as she prays. Sometimes she will say at once that she has a picture, so that we can all share the insight; but at other times she will refrain. From time to time when she and I have been praying together, Liz will say afterwards, 'I had a picture of such-and-such as we were praying about that problem. Does that help?' And, when I think about it, I find that her picture does indeed shed light on whatever problem we were bringing to God. However, had Liz told me during the prayer time I might have found it harder to take in just then.

Pictures that come from God may be prophetic, they may be a warning, or they may be something God wants an individual personally to hear and learn. When I first became a Christian, other important commitments made it impossible to join in all the activities that took place in my very large and busy church, which had a very big missionary and ministry service both in the UK and beyond. I longed to go to the prayer meetings, the missionary meetings, to help with this and assist in that. I felt, wrongly, of course, that because I wasn't involved I wasn't a 'proper' Christian, that I hadn't given my life fully to God.

Then God gave me a wonderful picture, which has proved not only encouraging and affirming but also prophetic. I saw a large walled orchard with row upon row of very fruitful apple trees. Everyone was busy picking apples, putting them in boxes and sending them off to distant parts of the world. I saw the orchard as my church, full of fruit and assiduously sending it out. Outside the wall was bleak moorland. A stony path wound through the rocks, and near that path stood a wind-swept, lone apple tree. It wasn't a young tree, but it had put its roots deep down in the poor soil and nothing would shift it. Its apples were hanging from the branches, and were gratefully taken by thirsty strangers as they passed by. This tree was me. I was of necessity 'outside' the church in that I couldn't take part in internal activities; but my fruit was there for others who needed it. God had a use for me.

I found this enormously comforting. It didn't matter that I couldn't do what everyone else did. God had a place for me, even if it felt a bit lonely at times. Later, I became involved with writing Bible notes for Scripture Union, and I still contribute to *Daily Bread*.

My fruit continues to be picked by passers-by who are unknown to me.

God may sometimes give us a word or picture that relates to the future. Caroline and Adam were in no doubt at all that the pictures they saw as they were praying together were from God. They each had identical images, quite independently of the other. Their friendship had developed into something deep and strong, and marriage was a definite possibility. As they were praying together one evening, each saw a vine with two branches twisted together, making one strong, bonded branch. But it was only strong because both branches came from the same root. They felt that this was a picture for them of the strong Christian marriage they could enjoy, and that God was telling them they were right for each other.

Just for you?

If you are unsure whether your pictures are meant for you alone, or are given to you by God for others, you need to ask God to tell you. For myself, I feel an enormous unease in my stomach when something is from God, and I can sense the Holy Spirit nudging and pushing me to get up and speak out. I feel no peace until I have done so. It wasn't always like that. When I first became a Christian, I was amazed at how many people in a meeting would get up and say they had 'a picture from God'. I never had pictures. Why were they so in touch with God and not me? (You will already have gathered from the earlier chapters that humility has not been an easy fruit for me to acquire!) Very gradually, as I began to mature as a

Christian, I realised that God *was* giving me pictures. At first, though, they were pictures for me alone; but occasionally I received a picture I felt was for others.

One weekend some years ago, about 200 people from my church went away to Ashburnham Place in Sussex for a church weekend. I was delighted to be able to go, but felt rather lonely and low as everyone else was part of a couple or a family. The teaching was excellent, but I was finding things all a bit too much. I thought, in my typically self-pitying way, that everyone else was having a wonderful time and I was all alone. As I walked in the beautiful grounds very early on the Sunday morning, I came to a closed and narrow path through some rhododendrons. Immediately, my mind filled with a picture of a jungle surrounding me and hemming me in with huge trees, tropical ferns and vines. Then I saw a machete clearing the ground in front of my feet so that I could take a step forward. As I stepped forward, the machete cleared another bit of ground for my next step. As I took another step, another bit of ground was cleared, and so on, till I could see the end of the path. I understood God to be telling me (I can't honestly say that I heard him speak – it was more a feeling) that I had to keep walking; that I didn't have to see the end before I started; that, as I stepped out in faith, he would clear the ground before me a bit at a time. It was no good standing still or I would be overwhelmed by the jungle.

This picture really impressed me and has been a blessing over the years in all sorts of difficult situations. When I shared it at the end of our weekend together, I found that two or three other people felt it was for them too. To my ashamed surprise, others had found the weekend difficult. Not everyone was having a wonderful time!

Don't despise your own pictures. Let your imagination flow as you read God's word. Learn from them. If the images seem particularly vivid or special, write them down (or draw or paint, if that is your gift). Ask God to make the meaning clear. If you feel they are for others to share, then speak up. Your leaders should be able to allow the group to think and pray about the picture and arrive at the deeper meaning.

Picture imperfect

Not everyone has a vivid imagination that can fly into distant realms. Some people are more down-to-earth and focus on the practicalities of life and faith. Both perspectives are essential. Unrealistic flights of fancy need to be earthed so as to bring us closer to what the Bible is actually saying. Yet our imaginations need to be unlocked so that we can explore symbolism and imagery. It is important that we don't fly off to the heights of imaginative fancies: that way lies heresy and a faith based on experience, not the word of God. But neither should we go to the opposite extreme of legalism and religiosity: that way is the way of the Pharisees.

Don't assume that everything in your mind is from God. Our minds are usually cluttered with the minutiae of daily living, and we can easily allow ourselves to let our worries and concerns take over and set our imaginations to work on them. In the same way, we can take hold of a situation and construct scenarios that seem very clear, but in reality are just our over-heated imaginations working. We are so eager to see ahead, to find out what is 'round the next corner', that we leap ahead, taking no account of the biblical perspective, the surrounding factors or the perceptions of others who may be wiser than we are. The ability to laugh at ourselves when we get like that is a wonderful antidote.

Anyone who has read and laughed over Adrian Plass's books will remember the bizarre 'pictures' involving, for example, aardvarks and jellyfish! I, for one, found them hugely funny, as I know thousands of others did. But the reason we found them so hilarious is because there is more than a grain of truth in what he wrote. Many people do try to 'spiritualise' everything their imaginations churn up, and much time can be wasted trying to find deep meanings in what was just a mental blip. We need to apply both discernment and plain common sense to what we picture in our minds.

Show me your ways, O Lord,
    teach me your paths;
guide me in your truth and teach me,
    for you are God my Saviour,
and my hope is in you all day long.

(Psalm 25:4–5)

Chapter 5

DREAMS AND VISIONS

The Hebrew of the Old Testament and the Greek of the New Testament both use one term to describe a dream and another, quite different term to describe a vision. However, the defining line between the two is rather nebulous. What we might think of as a dream can be called a vision, and vice versa. 'I have a dream,' declared Martin Luther King, meaning that he had a vision in his head of a multi-racial society living in peace together. Christians have a vision for their church, meaning that their minds are picturing packed churches, universal repentance and revival. These sorts of dreams or visions are within our conscious control. They are what we would like to see happen, what we plan and pray towards. But dreams and visions where God speaks to us are outside of our conscious control. We cannot plan for God to speak to us in our dreams, nor can we construct a vision to appear before our eyes.

As a rough guide to the difference between dreams and visions, I have taken dreams to be what we see when we are asleep, while visions are supernatural, highly intensified pictures or scenes that occur while we are awake.

Perchance to dream

Sleeping and dreaming are strange areas of our lives that even today scientists and psychologists do not fully understand. It appears that we all dream, and that dreaming sleep is vital to our physical and emotional health. During dreaming sleep, our brains are more active than when we are awake, dealing with our fears, anxieties and what has been happening to us, so that it can be safely 'filed away' in our subconscious.

Our dreams can be weird, wonderful and out of this world, or worrying, unsettling and incomprehensible. They can be vague, shadowy remembrances, or vivid pictures that stay with us for months or even years. They can be 'one-offs', or recurring dreams where we are in the same place or doing the same thing again and again.

The meanings of dreams

I have an old book, *The Every Woman's Enquire Within*, published in the late 1920s, which devotes a whole section to the meanings of dreams. Apparently if you dream of cutting your finger, it means you will be involved in a law suit. Dreaming of garden flowers is bad, though 'dandelions are very auspicious'! Mice mean bankruptcy and zebras a long life. All this nonsense was contradicted in a recently published book by a well-known astrologer and fortune-teller. This time round, mice mean family rows and zebras mean a surprise gain. A cut finger means a lot of hard work and all flowers are good. Dandelions seem to have disappeared as a meaningful dream symbol. It's a pity – they are more resilient in my garden!

If it is foolish to try to interpret our own dreams in this way, it is even more foolish to try to interpret the dreams of others. It is equally unwise to assume that all dreams come from God – they don't. Trying to find a spiritual meaning in every dream may have damaging consequences. More often than not, dreams arise from the subconscious workings of our minds, from our own worries and insecurities, from events of the day, from what the hot-and-spicy pizza is doing to our digestion! Jeremiah understood this and censured those false prophets who represented the workings of their subconscious minds as messages from God (Jer 23:16–29).

However, *some* dreams *do* come from God. During our dreaming sleep, when we are not so beset by the distractions of our daytime lives, would seem a good time for God to speak into our minds. The Bible gives many instances of men and women hearing from God through dreams. Joseph was urged in a dream to take Mary as his wife even though she was pregnant (Matt 1:20); later, he was warned to flee with the baby Jesus and Mary to Egypt, to escape the coming slaughter by Herod (2:13). The wise men were warned in a dream to return to their country by another route (2:12). Interestingly, God can reach us through our dreams even if we do not believe in him. Pharaoh had dreams from God (Gen 41), and Pilate's wife dreamed about Jesus (Matt 27:19).

How can I tell which dreams are from God?

Sleep scientists assure us that we all dream during periods of lighter sleep which occur regularly throughout the night, but we only remember those dreams that take place just before awakening. Even then, many of our dreams remain shadowy, slipping through the fingers of our minds as we try to grasp them. Many people, whether Christian or not, like to keep a notebook and pencil handy by the bed to write their dreams down the minute they wake up. This may be OK if you wake up at a sensible hour, full of bounce and energy, and have a compliant sleeping partner! It is not a lot of help to those of us who wake during the night. Putting on the light and sitting up in bed to write in the wee small hours does not make for a happy spouse. Neither does it make it easy to get back to sleep, and the disturbance to our sleep patterns may be counter-productive healthwise. Anyone who has had disturbed nights with a sick child will know how debilitating such disturbed sleep can be.

Nor is all this necessary. I don't believe God would speak to us in a way we cannot remember. As well as being a God of love, compassion and faithfulness, he is a God of logic and order. All the dreams described in the Bible have been clear and lucid, and the details have stayed with the dreamer long after waking. In Genesis 40, both the baker and the cupbearer were able to recount their dreams of the night before for Joseph to interpret. Nebuchadnezzar remembered his dreams for quite some time before Daniel gave him their meaning (Dan 2,4). Why should we be any different?

A vivid dream may well be from God, if all or most of the details remain clear in your mind on waking, and stay there for some time after you have got up and attended to the distractions of the morning. It is at this point (perhaps during your early morning time with God, if you have one) that it is helpful to write down, as best you can, what you have dreamed. It is not always easy. Dreams seem to happen in several dimensions. Things, places, events and people change as we dream, defying chronology and earthly sense. You may even have problems putting what you have seen into words. (I have a great deal of sympathy for John as he struggled to write coherently about his fantastic revelation!) But it is worth trying.

Once the general outline of your dream is down on paper and not likely to be lost in the hurly-burly of life, you can then try to understand what God is saying. Does the dream refer to something you have been worrying about? Could it hold an answer to prayer? Does it contain a warning about something you were contemplating doing? Is there a definite yes or no in it? If you can't see anything that makes sense, the dream may not be from God. If you can't fathom it out but still feel strongly that the dream is from God, ask him to confirm whether this is so. Tell him that you don't understand and humbly invite him to make things plainer.

Frightening dreams

Sometimes we have weird, frightening dreams that are incredibly vivid. They don't quite come under the heading of nightmares, but they are disturbing and worrying, and seem to infect us with a sense of foreboding or even evil. Contrary to normal dreams which disappear as fast as we try to remember them, these dreams are hard to forget. There are probably many reasons why we have such dreams. They could be the effect of medication or of traumatic events in our lives, or they might have a spiritual source other than God.

I suffer from this sort of dream myself and have found that one or two have indeed been a warning from God. I have found that the best way to differentiate between these dreams is to pray. I tell God how much they bother me and ask him to take away the memory of these dreams if they are not from him, to wipe them from my mind. Once or twice I have felt certain that they have had a satanic origin, and have stood firmly against Satan and told him to go, to get out of my mind: 'Resist the devil, and he will flee from you' (James 4:7), though he may well try to come back. If I have been having these dreams every night or so, I have found it helpful to pray before I go to sleep, asking God to protect my mind. I have to say, however, that, as far as my personal experience goes, dreams like this are usually a permanent side-effect of medication and it may be that we just have to live with them. If you are on necessary, long-term medication which has this effect, you will have to find a way to overcome them.

Some years before I became a Christian, I was suffering very badly from deep clinical depression. Suicidal thoughts were never far from my mind. I came from a totally non-Christian, unchurched family, and knew no one who was a believer. One night I had a very intense dream, every frightening detail of which, over fifteen years later, is still with me. It was this dream which convinced me I needed medical help, urgently and immediately – help which enabled me to regain my sanity and balance. What I saw in my dream was the first real intimation I had received that there really was a God and that death did not result in annihilation or nothingness. Looking back, I know now that God gave me a warning of where my life was heading and my ultimate destiny if I didn't do something.

But we can have frightening dreams even when we are Christians. Twenty-five years ago, when my friend Vera was a very new Christian, she started having terrifying dreams of hideous faces looming over her. In her dream she called out to Jesus for help, because he was all she had. Being such a new Christian, she knew of no one she could talk to or who might support her with prayer. The dreams lasted three long nights, and Vera felt that if she hadn't known Jesus as her Saviour she would have cracked up. On the fourth night she had another dream of a shining cross. Jesus stood underneath it, wearing a glowing cloak. She heard the most beautiful heavenly music and felt God's presence. She woke up and was very aware that the peace of God filled the bedroom. After that, the evil dreams ceased. Vera still doesn't know why she had them, but she does know that Jesus is stronger than anything our unconscious minds can bring forth.

We should not neglect our dreams, as God can and does speak to us. If we are resistant to his voice in our waking life, it may be the only way he can reach us.

Visions

We all dream while we are asleep, but not everyone has visions, those 'waking dreams' which have a base in reality. Visions usually arise out of what we see, but are transformed by God to give us a prophecy, a warning, an instruction or encouragement.

When he was in Troas, Paul had a vision of a man from Macedonia begging him to help the people in that country (Acts 16:8–10). Luke, who wrote Acts, was with Paul in Troas, and he is quite clear that Paul did not have a dream. Luke does not use the usual Greek word for 'dream'; rather, he uses the word which is translated as 'sight' or 'spectacle', the same word as that found in Acts 7:31, for example, when Stephen describes the burning bush seen by Moses. Paul had a vision, not a dream.

We can't make visions happen any more than we can control our dreams, but if we want to hear God speaking to us in the many ways he uses, we need to be aware of what is happening around us. To put everything down to imagination is wrong. However, it is just as unhelpful to block your imagination off completely.

Visions, especially those on a grand scale, may be just for you, but perhaps more often they are for a church or fellowship, whether large or small. If this is the case, it is wise to take your vision first to the leadership before standing up in a meeting and declaring, 'I have a vision!' If the vision is for a wider group and truly from God, then it is up to the leaders to decide whether to act or to ignore it, as the case may be.

Margaret was a member of a very large church in the Midlands. She was aware of rumours of disagreement among the leadership, and knew that dissension had surfaced among members at the church meetings, but nothing had seemed very serious.

One sunny day, as she went blackberrying in the local woods, she had a very strange experience. Where she was walking the undergrowth was mainly ivy. It covered the ground and had started to climb up the trees where, in one or two places, it was seriously damaging the trees' growth. As she wandered along the path, the wood became the church, the trees forming a sort of human structure. Sin and dissension, like the ivy, were beginning to strangle the growth God wanted to see. As she walked further, she came to an older, more neglected part of the wood where the ivy had killed many trees, but they were still standing, giving the appearance of life. The ground shrubs were totally strangled and there was no new growth. As Margaret looked at this, she knew that she was looking at the future of her beloved fellowship.

Feeling very strongly that the presence of God was there, she paused. Then she saw, at a distance from where she was standing, a part of the wood that was familiar to her. There the trees were free of ivy and growing robustly, reaching up to the sky. Young trees sprang up strongly, growing well in the protection of the older trees. This was what God wanted her fellowship to be.

Margaret remained standing in the middle of the wood, unaware of anything around her and feeling totally divorced from reality, until the vision faded and she felt herself again. She was unsure what to do. If she kept her vision to herself, then what was the point of God giving it to her? If she went up to one of the leaders and told him what she had seen, even if she could relate it in a coherent and sensible manner, he would probably just say, 'Yes, yes! How interesting', and leave it at that. In the end, she wrote down what she had seen as clearly as she could and took it to the leader she knew best, explaining how it had all come about. He took Margaret seriously and read out her vision to the other leaders at their next meeting. It was received in silence. The challenge to change, to root out the dissension and sin was not taken up. A few months later, the leadership problems led to a serious and permanent rift in the church. About a third of the members left, and it took many, many months for healing and restoration to begin to take place.

What should Margaret have done? What would you have done? How would your own church or fellowship have received such a vision? How can those in leadership help ordinary members to have confidence in listening to God? In his first letter to the Corinthians, Paul is very clear that all should be able to say what they have heard from God and should be listened to with respect (1 Cor 14:26,31). However we hear God speaking to us, it is *his* word. If we are merely the bearers of his message, we need to feel confident that those for whom God intends it will hear it.

Visions such as Margaret had are not easy to deal

with and it is wise to pray about them first before making them public. As with dreams, if you feel they really are for your fellowship group or church, then ask God to confirm this. Visions are not just bigger and better pictures; they are reality transformed. They are often God saying something important on a grand scale. We need to give them the attention they demand.

Chapter 6

THE WORLD AROUND US

It was barely light when the dog and I set off, rather earlier than usual, for our morning walk. Normally we went into the wood, but I was feeling a bit wary. It seemed so very dark and I could scarcely see the trees.

As we approached the wood I noticed, with some surprise, that against the dark mass the trunks of the silver birches shone quite brightly in the half-light. There was no way their gleaming, straight forms were going to merge into the dim, anonymous background. They seemed almost like graceful beacons showing me the way. Then God spoke into my heart, 'Do you shine like that for me against a dark world?'

'Do I?' I pondered as I walked carefully along the dark path. 'Do I seem any different from the non-Christians around me? Can they see that my godly standards are perhaps different from theirs? Could I, should I, stand out more, like those silver birches?'

When God speaks to me through his creation, he very often seems to be in teaching mode. This isn't surprising when you think about it – we have already seen that Jesus himself used examples from the natural world to demonstrate godly truths. He encouraged his disciples to look around them and learn. 'Consider the ravens,' he said. 'Consider how the lilies grow' (Luke 12:24,27). When Jesus says, 'Consider', he is saying, 'Look carefully and learn from.' This is no superficial glance; we need to open our hearts and minds as well as our eyes to see what the world around us can teach us.

Hundreds of years earlier, the writers of the Bible's wisdom literature understood this need to observe creation with insight:

When I consider your heavens,
    the work of your fingers,
the moon and the stars,
    which you have set in place,
what is man that you are mindful of him,
    the son of man that you care for him?

(Psalm 8:3–4)

The psalmist looked to the heavens to grasp something of the greatness of God and to wonder at his love for us human beings, who are so small in comparison. We too might see mountains, a sunset, the raging of the sea, and feel similar awe. The writer of Proverbs, on the other hand, examined the small things of life:

Go to the ant, you sluggard;
    consider its ways and be wise!
It has no commander,
    no overseer or ruler,
yet it stores its provisions in summer

and gathers its food at harvest.

(Proverbs 6:6-8)

It doesn't matter whether they are big things or small, everything has the potential to be God's voice to us.

Real learning

We don't all hear God speak to us through our surroundings all the time, but few of us are totally impervious. Most of us can appreciate a majestic landscape, a spectacular sunrise or a beautiful garden. Local beauty spots are popular precisely because they are beautiful and worth visiting for their charm, spectacular scenery or peaceful location. We all can, and hopefully do, praise God for his wonderful creation, but to hear what he is saying to us we need to open our eyes and ears, to be receptive and prepared to learn. We need a quality of observation and a curiosity that, as adults, we may lack. Children, on the other hand, are naturally curious. They ask questions and often see things that grown-ups miss or with which we have become overfamiliar. To see God's hand and hear his voice in the world around us, we may need to abandon our 'seen that, done that' attitude and become 'like a little child' (Mark 10:15).

However, it is not always the case that we ignore our surroundings because of their overfamiliarity. In our busy world, our minds may be so full of other matters and concerns, we cannot take in any more; our eyes merely see enough to prevent us literally walking into disaster. God may well bring something to our attention and our reaction is, 'Oh yes, very nice', and we dismiss it because we have no room in our heads to consider it further.

There are two questions we should be asking ourselves as we observe and ponder what we see.

• What is God saying about himself, or about his laws or commands?

• What is God saying to me, personally?

One day, as I was driving along a narrow lane, I rather suddenly met one of those big, tractor-driven, mechanical hedge-trimmers. It chugged along, its huge blade ripping and tearing the hedge into a shredded mess. Sometimes, I thought, my life feels a bit like that – battered and shredded and left in a tangle of confusion. I remembered the hedges bordering a big house in our village – so neat and thick, as perfect as a hedge could be. They, of course, had a professional gardener. As I pondered this, I began to think how much better our lives would be if we let our heavenly Father be our professional gardener (John 15:1). He might cut off just as much as the mechanical cutter did from the hedge, but the result would be a million times better. If we don't want to be battered and ripped apart by life, perhaps we would do well to offer ourselves to God's pruning knife. No ripping and tearing, leaving gaping wounds, for him.

God showed me this illustration of Jesus' teaching in John 15 in a way that was vivid and easy to remember, but I had to dig deeper and use my mind to discover what he was saying to me. I had at times felt very much like a battered hedge, but I needed to think over my own life and see if there were any badly growing bits that I could give to God to clean up. There were, of course. Perhaps that was why God had arranged for the hedgecutter to be just there, at that time.

Tongues in trees, sermons in stones

As we saw in the previous chapter, Jesus taught his followers using imagery with which they would have been familiar. Should we be surprised if God uses the things that are familiar to us in order to teach us?

One summer morning I was out walking the dog, when a sudden sharp shower caught me unawares. Luckily there was a large oak tree nearby, and the dog and I sheltered under it. I was saying, 'Thank you, Lord, for oak trees', when I started to look at it more closely. We were sheltered from the rain because the leaves were flat, their surfaces facing upwards. Not only that, the leaves were spread out, each trying to catch the sun, so that from underneath the tree looked like a huge umbrella. This, of course, is what leaves need to do to get sunlight, to initiate the process of photosynthesis and thus give life to the tree. Only as a secondary consideration does this result in shelter for man and his animals.

Then I realised that this is true for us also. If we do not look towards God, seeking him as a leaf seeks light, then we will not function properly. Our ministries, great or small, depend totally on our seeking God first (Matt 6:33). If we fail to put God first and think only of our own agenda and our own glory, then however successful our ministries are, they will not be anointed by the Holy Spirit. This applies whether we try to sit unnoticed at the back or participate in the main action up front. Those who put themselves, their status and their reputation first are those of whom Jesus was speaking when he said these awesome and frightening words:

'Not everyone who says to me, "Lord, Lord,"
will enter the kingdom of heaven, but only he
who does the will of my Father who is in
heaven. Many will say to me on that day,
"Lord, Lord, did we not prophesy in your
name, and in your name drive out demons and
perform many miracles?" Then I will tell them
plainly, "I never knew you. Away from me, you
evildoers!" '

(Matthew 7:21–23)

When I ran for cover that summer day I already knew these verses, of course, but it took a bit of rain and an oak tree to drive their truth deep into me.

The Pennine landscape after a winter snowfall is a very black-and-white affair. White fields are criss-crossed by the black lines of dry-stone walls that straddle the snowy moors. There is no room for greys here. Even in the valleys the farms are black and white. Dark slate roofs are set in snowy yards dotted with black tracks. Sheep huddle in the shelter of the stone walls, resignation on their inky faces.

I was gazing at such a landscape one winter's day when it occurred to me that this is how God sees sin.

When it comes to sin, there are no 'greys' with him. He does not excuse sin, pat us on the head and say, 'There, there, it doesn't matter.' He took our sin so seriously, he sent his own Son to die for us. Only through Jesus' death as atonement for our sin was God then able to look upon us, his sinful children, and forgive us. That bitter, harsh, black-and-white moorland landscape spoke very strongly to me.

> And this our life, exempt from public haunt,
> Finds tongues in trees, books in the running
>   brooks,
> Sermons in stones, and good in everything.

(Shakespeare, As You like it, Act II)

God can use anything as a visual aid

It is not just through the world of nature that we hear God. Everything, if we open our minds, can be used by God.

The morning after Bonfire Night, our garden was littered with empty firework cases and the sticks from rockets which had come from neighbouring gardens. 'What a waste,' I thought. (I'm not a lover of fireworks!) 'All that money spent on a few seconds of bangs, colour and lights, and nothing left afterwards but old cardboard and a few sticks.' Then I realised that we can all be like that: all keen for Jesus one minute; then our first enthusiasm dies down and we become dead and ineffective. God wants us to burn with a steady light, fuelled by the mains of his power and love. So many people commit themselves to

Jesus in a burst of enthusiasm, then drop away as the fire goes out and they fall to the ground.

On a visit to Paris, Sylvia was sitting in a restaurant on the Boulevard St Michel, staring out at the frantic traffic and the preoccupied passers-by. She felt it was all fake; they were *poseurs*, not real. Later, she saw several crippled beggars whose humility and plight touched her deeply. These people, she felt God say to her, are the significant ones when seen with his eyes, not the eyes of the world. Our pretences and arrogance do not fool God. His eyes see us as we really are and we cannot hide ourselves from him.

It's not all teaching

Besides teaching us, God can also offer us reassurance, comfort and encouragement.

Jenny had her own special prayer spot which she would drive to. One day as she parked the car, she noticed an old, gnarled, very dead tree trunk surrounded by weeds and brambles. Out of the trunk was growing a yellow tulip. Jenny was amazed that this flower could grow in such a seemingly impossible situation. As she contemplated it, she sensed that the Lord was speaking to her about someone for whom she had been praying a long time.

The tulip could only have grown from a seed, as no one could have planted a bulb in that space. This seed represented the seed of God's word, which he plants in our hearts. The seed takes time to grow, in this case into a bulb, before it will even begin to produce a flower. But here, before her eyes, she saw the finished product. The leaves were a little bit slug-eaten, showing that its growth had not been smooth; but the flower itself was perfect. To Jenny, it represented the golden crown that all the saints of God are given. She felt that, through the tulip, God was giving her strong encouragement to believe that what she was praying for would be fulfilled. When the situation seems hopeless, she holds on to that picture, as she knows God is faithful.

Using all our senses

Though we see God's creation with our eyes, it is also there for us to hear and feel.

Chris was in a very difficult church situation, facing a potentially explosive meeting with her minister. A couple of hours before the interview, she walked along to the centre of her quiet, west country village and found a bench on the green to sit on. As she sat there, she began to be aware of the breeze rustling the leaves of the trees around her. Some leaves produced a high, soft sound, while the leaves of the thick holly tree behind her added the bass notes. It was like a beautiful symphony. As Chris listened to the harmony of the leaves blown by the wind, she felt the utter peace of God blown into her being by the Holy Spirit. God had given her the 'peace that passes all understanding'. Though the interview proved worse than she imagined, God's 'symphony of peace' remained.

Danger

God's creation is good, but we live in a fallen world. Not everything is godly. It would be all too easy, when we think we hear God speak to us, to misunderstand what he is saying. For example, we could draw from the tenacity of something like bindweed the message that God wants us to climb all over weaker people and overwhelm them! We need to check the message out. Is it biblical? Is it loving? Another danger is that we venerate the creation rather than the Creator. A special spot or tree, say, becomes an idol to which we return again and again, trying to hear God speak once more in the same way. I have always been very aware that this is not what God wants.

Some time ago, in a scruffy clearing, I came upon a very ordinary clump of flowering grass growing among a tangle of brambles and fallen branches. Suddenly a stray sunbeam highlighted the grass and it was immediately transformed. The graceful, delicate flower heads were clusters of minute bells, their stalks swaying gently in the wind, while the sword-like leaves fell in perfect symmetry around them. My breath was taken away by the exquisite, unexpected loveliness in that very lowly place. We are all like that, I realised, when we turn towards Jesus and the light of his love shines on our lives. It is this love that transforms us, as the sunbeam transformed the grass.

Although that clump of grass was very close to my regular walk through the wood, I was never able to find it again. I was quite a young Christian at the time and, looking back, I could easily have thought, 'God is here. If I come back, I will find him again.'

We must also beware of slipping into the belief that our special place is the *only* place we will hear God. It can be very helpful to have a special place to pray in – a place where we can quieten our minds and come more easily into God's presence, whether this is in the countryside, the corner of a room or even a particular chair. For many Christians, it is easier to concentrate our thoughts on God if we are alone and quiet, and for some that may well mean finding a place apart somewhere. But not everyone can do this, or needs to. God is everywhere. His voice can reach us wherever we are, whether at home with young children, on a crowded commuter train or in the factory, office or shop. We do not need to have total silence, or be in a special place or in contact with a special object.

Over to you

Why not take time over the next few days and weeks to really look at the world around you? Not just the natural things, the smallest flowers and the greatest hills: look also at the people, the joys and sadnesses of childhood, the faces of older folk. Think of the land, the way we use and misuse it. Open your eyes and your ears. What can you smell or feel? God wants to speak to you. Ask him what he is saying, and what he is saying to you in particular.

God saw all that he had made, and it was very good.

(Genesis 1:31)

Chapter 7

HEARING GOD THROUGH PAIN

Suffering comes to us in various forms, physically, mentally, emotionally and spiritually. Each form is so different, we cannot say which is worse. Who, for example, could rate the pain of a kidney stone against the loss of a child? The two are not comparable. But each brings agony of body and of mind, which in turn affects the emotions and the spirit. We are made as an integrated whole; if one part of us suffers, then the rest is out of kilter. Pain, for whatever reason, has the effect of distorting our balance, disrupting the way we feel, behave and think. Severe pain can dominate our whole existence and, in our natural desire to avoid or control it, we may let it block our ears to God's voice.

Which of us has not felt our ability to pray dwindle away in the presence of pain? Which of us has not felt that our prayers for relief are banging against the closed doors of heaven?

My God, my God, why have you forsaken me?
    Why are you so far from saving me,
      so far from the words of my groaning?
O my God, I cry out by day, but you do not
      answer,

by night, and am not silent.

> *(Psalm 22:1–2)*

Answer me, O Lord, out of the goodness of
    your love;
in your great mercy turn to me.
Do not hide your face from your servant;
    answer me quickly, for I am in trouble.

> *(Psalm 69:16–17)*

While psalms like these may reflect the psalmist's
anguish, bewilderment and despair, each one also
shows his firm, underlying belief that God is there
and that he is faithful.

Why am I so sad?
    Why am I so troubled?
I will put my hope in God,
    and once again I will praise him,
    my saviour and my God.

> *(Psalm 42:11, GNB)*

I have drawn tremendous encouragement from Jane
Grayshon's books, in which she describes her experience of years of pain. For over twenty years she
suffered from chronic abdominal infections that peri-
odically erupted into acute, life threatening illness.
Several times she was on the brink of death.

Jane struggled to understand why God would allow
her to go through such unbearable and continuous
pain. She felt God was asking too much of her. People

told her that she gave enormous help to others through her books and her speaking engagements, but even that did not seem a good reason for so much suffering. Eventually, agonisingly, over the long years, the hundreds of wakeful, pain-filled hours, and bitter disappointment that God neither healed her nor permitted her to die, Jane came to accept her situation. She realised that she was so busy focusing on what she wanted God to do for her, she had lost sight of who he is and what he had already done. What God had given her was more valuable than the healing of the body.

God is good. His purposes are for good and not for evil. His ways are not our ways. We don't know why he allows hard and painful things, but neither do we know why we receive his blessings. Neither are earned, and both are God's gifts.

I have no doubt that pain is a thief, a robber. I have watched it cling like a leech to people – patients I have nursed, friends, spouses of colleagues – and it has sucked their very lifeblood until they have been dead, yet left carrying the intolerable burden of their body. I have listened to men weep great sobs as they have talked of pain stealing away the laughter from their marriage – and not just the laughter. It is the very soul of a person that pain grips; it lynches the personality, draining away hope until all one is left with is the wretchedness of a body too exhausted to love.

Pain is a thief and a robber, stealing souls from bodies and minds.

Pain is also a gift. It transports people from remote independence to vulnerable dependence. It transforms from hard know-alls to stumbling questors. Therefore we hate it: we have to learn how to do otherwise. It leads us into awareness of our need for God. When it persists or burns more fiercely it makes us shout in prayer at the God Who seems not to have heard us. He can't have heard if He isn't doing something! And as our shouts grow louder and the pain remains we are forced to listen to our prayers.

To hear our prayers is a gift which silences our loud self-orientation and opens the door to let us hear how our Saviour is praying.

If pain goes on yet more; if it goes on beyond what we feel we can bear, we have no option other than to look at the darkness and face what is happening to us and in us. That is when we enter the process of healing. For healing is not an event, but a process. And pain can be the vehicle, not the enemy.

(Jane Grayshon, Treasures of Darkness, *1996, reproduced by permission of Hodder and Stoughton Limited)*

Jennifer Rees Larcombe suffered from repeated attacks of encephalitis and, on at least four occasions, had been on the point of death. Each attack left her progressively weaker and more disabled. She desperately sought healing. Was it a question of mind-over-matter, positive thinking, more faith, or what?

One day, struggling obstinately to go for a walk by herself, Jenny's sticks slipped and she fell down in a muddy, cow-ridden morass. As she lay there weeping, she railed furiously at God. It seemed to her that the state she was in was just like her life – messy, unpleasant and out of control. Then, as tears of anger mingled with the filth, she heard God answering her – not in a voice nor in words, but she knew without any doubt at all that he cared intensely about the mess her life was in. He would be there with her, if only she didn't keep pushing him away. Jenny was astounded, but began to think. Had she made what she wanted more important than anything else? Had her desire for healing and independence become her god? Slowly, Jenny began to accept her disability and the restrictions of her life, though she continued to feel frustration at her immobility and helplessness. Then, one glorious day, she was brought healing by a young, diffident and hurting Christian.

Roy and Fiona Castle and their family were much-loved members of my first church. When Roy was first diagnosed with cancer of the lung, there was a great deal of prayer for his recovery. But Roy's illness was news and, in addition to facing the pain and trauma of his illness, they had to endure the pressures of the media. However, Fiona and Roy were sure that God would use their circumstances if they would only let him do so. Fiona felt that God was saying, 'Stand back and see what I will do through this.'

Roy himself had complete confidence in God, even in his darkest and most painful moments. Fiona told me that he would pray, 'This isn't the way I would have chosen. But if this is the way you want it, Lord, then that's OK by me.' God gave Roy glimpses of the world to come: a beautiful, perfect garden; amazing lights in unimaginable colours. 'Don't hang around, darling,' he told Fiona. 'This is too good to miss.' He died full of faith and trust in the goodness of God.

Fiona has never lost this unshakeable faith that God is good. She draws strength and comfort from the words of Oswald Chambers: 'If through a broken heart God can use you, then let your heart break, and thank him'. For a time it felt as though there were no more questions she could ask God, no more prayers she could offer up to him. She learnt to stop asking God for things, and to acknowledge his goodness and sovereignty.

When you are hurting, you need to give God that hurt. Never say, 'I shouldn't be feeling like this; other people's pain is far greater than mine.' This may well be true (though who can grade pain?), but if we are truly hurting, and not just feeling self-pity, then that hurt to us is as important as it feels.

My own emotional pain has in no way ever been comparable to what others have suffered. Yet in his infinite graciousness God has given me peace, encouragement and a deep joy. One blissful day I managed to get away for a day alone with God in a beautiful old house set high in the hills above the Thames. I was given a small room all to myself, and was able to wander freely in the beautiful gardens. In the room was a small 'prayer corner' with a simple cross, a prayer stool and a candle on a little table. Towards the end of my time there I lit the candle, but the late afternoon sun streamed in the window and I could scarcely see the flame. As I stared at it, I felt God speak to me: 'My love for you is as steadfast as a candle flame in a still room. It will never waver and will never end. When the sun is shining, you cannot see the flame. But when all is dark, the flame brings light to the whole room. My flame will never be extinguished.'

> 'I will give you the treasures of darkness,
>   riches stored in secret places,
> so that you may know that I am the Lord...'
>
> *(Isaiah 45:3)*

Without the darkness, we cannot see the light. Without the darkness, we will not find the treasure.

Kelly struggled with her tears as she manoeuvred the pushchair around the puddles on her way to the day nursery. How could God ask her to stay in this situation? How could she stay, when each day seemed to bring more rows, more rejection, more hurt?

The morning was very still. The rain had stopped, but every leaf, every blade of grass glistened. As Kelly passed under the hanging branches of a larch tree, she saw that each tiny needle held a rain drop. The whole branch shone as though hung with diamonds.

Then, in the depths of her mind, she heard God say, 'Give me your tears, and I will make them into a necklace of jewels.'

That was all. Kelly needed no more. God was not going to take her out of the situation, but somehow transform it. Tears and hurt would remain, but God would take them and make them into something good.

God allows pain and suffering for reasons beyond our comprehension. For Fiona and Roy Castle, Jennifer Rees Larcombe and Jane Grayshon, only the acceptance of God's goodness and sovereignty, however hard that is, made any sense. When we give God our tears, our prayers, our distress and our suffering, we will find him. You may not find your 'necklace of jewels' this side of death – but find it you will.

'This isn't the way I would have chosen. But if that's the way you want it, Lord, then that's OK by me.'

Chapter 8

Λ WORD ΛPTLY SPOKEN

God does not always thunder from the skies, make Bible verses seemingly jump out of the page at us or overwhelm us with messages from his created world. He doesn't need to. We, as Christ's body, on earth should be his messengers, his voice, his hands, his feet. Often when we talk about ourselves as God's messengers, what we have in mind is proclaiming the good news of the gospel to a lost world. But God speaks to us not just for our salvation, but also for teaching, correcting and rebuking us as we grow as Christians (2 Tim 3:16).

In the early history of the Israelites, God spoke to his people through the men he had raised up as leaders. Abraham, Isaac and Jacob, and later Moses and Joshua all had a 'direct line' to God. Later on in the Old Testament, we discover that God spoke to the child Samuel as he called him to be his servant and spokesman. After that he generally spoke through the prophets, proclaiming his plans and his promises, voicing his displeasure and declaring his love for his people. The role of prophet was an important one; even David, that great man of God, needed the prophet Nathan to tell him of God's anger over his affair with Bathsheba (2 Sam 12). But God also used ordinary people. Naaman began his journey towards healing through the words of a young slave girl (2 Kings 5). Saul was persuaded to meet Samuel by his servant who, like Naaman's slave girl, is not named (1 Sam 9:5–10). Abigail, the hard-working wife of a rich but boorish landowner, prevented David from committing a bloodthirsty act of retaliation (1 Sam 25:23–34).

So God's messages to us do not have to come from the mouths of great speakers or preachers; they can come from anyone – family, friends, strangers, even those who are relatively young in faith. It is comforting and inspirational when someone brings us a word of encouragement 'from the Lord'. And, though we may be prepared to listen to a good teacher expound the Bible in a sermon or our Bible reading notes, it takes a good deal of humility to accept correction and rebuke from people who are frail human beings like ourselves.

Jane was a great worrier. She worried over big things and little things. She worried over where her children would go to school – and this was before she even became pregnant! She worried how many days she would be able to work when she was a mother. She worried about where she would park the car before she went anywhere. She had a very firm life-plan and she worried how she would complete it. She wasn't particularly bothered by all this worrying, though she did feel stressed. She felt it was quite natural to worry. How else would her life be organised and under control?

Jane hid her worries well. No one who knew her would have known that her mind was a turmoil of anxiety about things she had absolutely no control over.

One day she was praying with a friend and laying some of her concerns before God, when her friend asked, 'Jane, don't you think you worry too much?'

'Don't be ridiculous,' thought Jane. 'Of course I don't worry too much. I just need to make sure everything goes right.'

But God had spoken to Jane through those words of her friend, and it suddenly dawned on her how much she had been a captive to her own worry. There was actually no need for it – God was in control.

Sometimes Jane's anxiety returns, mostly when she is tired or stressed. Then she hears God say to her, 'Jane, you're worrying again!' And she consciously breaks the chain that is threatening her to bind her up once more.

In her book, *God's Gloves*, Jennifer Rees Larcombe tells of a woman whose first baby was desperately ill in a special care baby unit. She was crying as she travelled down in the lift from the ward.

A nurse, who was also in the lift, said to her, 'I can see that you're sad. Why not try praying about it?'

The doors of the lift opened and they never met again, but her words were imprinted on the mother's mind. She felt that she couldn't pray if she knew nothing about God, so she went to church, began reading Christian books and became a strong Christian. Those few words from a nurse changed her life.

Are you talking to me?

So, you have heard a good sermon, or received some good advice from a friend, but are still unsure that what you have heard is God's words for you, personally. How can you know?

When the great Charles Spurgeon preached in the Metropolitan Tabernacle at Newington Causeway in London, hundreds of people acknowledged their need for repentance before God and most of them made a commitment to Christ. Others had preached before him on similar subjects and in similar terms, but, to quote Principal Tulloch who was Spurgeon's contemporary, what was characteristic of his sermons were their 'power and life'. Well, like that description of Spurgeon's sermons, God's words will have power and life – power to cut straight to the heart and mind, and life to bring life, to answer questions, instruct or educate. The writer of Hebrews describes God's word as 'alive and active, sharper than any double-edged sword' (Heb 4:12, GNB). But this sword is no destructive implement, slashing and cutting indiscriminately; rather, it is more like a surgeon's knife, cutting out the bad and repairing the good.

Have you ever had something on your conscience, or felt 'out of sorts with God', then listened to the minister's sermon and thought it was directed straight at you? 'How did *he* know?' you wonder guiltily! Well, he doesn't, of course; it is God using his words to speak to you personally. It may well be that, as you discuss the sermon afterwards, you will find that others have not heard it exactly as you have. God has taken the words of his servant and given them special meaning for you, because that is what he wants to say to *you*.

A great speaker will inspire us and teach us more about God's word and about God himself. That, after all, is the whole purpose of a sermon or message. No good preacher or teacher wants his or her words forgotten and left in the pews along with the hymn books. But often a specific message from God seems to come almost as an aside, in a throw-away comment. The words themselves may not seem particularly meaningful and the speaker doesn't realise their significance for you, but, like the surgeon's knife, they have a powerful impact. They home in on you like a heat-seeking missile. They stick in your mind, bother and nag at you until you take them on board and deal with the situation.

When I was desperately seeking the right church in the town we had moved to, I became badly depressed and felt very dry and far from God. I just didn't seem to fit in anywhere or to be what others expected me to be. One Sunday morning, I went, for the first time, to a small church that some friends of mine attended. During his message Steve, the pastor, said, 'What would you do if Jesus came in that door now?' Probably this is a question many preachers have asked, but to me, at that time, it came straight from God. I felt Jesus affirm deep within my heart, 'It's OK to be you.' Steve's simple question, and God's answer, cleared my mind of all doubts. I knew I had found the right church. It wasn't what Steve said; it was how God used his words to answer my prayers, and answer them in a way I could not have imagined.

In the presence of his people

There is a special dynamic in being part of a group of worshipping Christians, where all hearts are as one, turned towards God in thanksgiving and praise. When we are with others, sometimes it seems the Holy Spirit is present in an awesomeness and power that rarely happens when we pray by ourselves.

You may feel that it is easier to hear God through the words of others if you go to a small church which has non-liturgical services and where everyone is encouraged to take an active, spontaneous part in the service and in church life. A word or prayer can be for everyone present and, at the same time, a specific message for one person. However, you don't have to attend a Pentecostal or especially charismatic church to hear God! He operates far beyond our denominational boundaries.

In a church in the north of England, Lindsey was known and appreciated for the words she occasionally brought from God during the meetings. One Sunday morning, she told the meeting she felt God was saying that the wedding was not the only new start; fresh starts were always available, and he was a God who makes everything new. It was the day after a big and happy wedding of two of their church members, and Lindsey knew that there were at least two couples expecting babies plus another two recent arrivals. But it was not just new babies and new marriages God was talking about: old marriages and broken family relationships could also be renewed and refreshed. This was received as an encouraging word by everyone – after all, we all feel sometimes that we'd like to go back to the beginning and do things differently. But one particular couple, who were only visiting the church and whose marriage was very shaky, knew that the words had been especially appropriate and challenging to them. They felt they could start to tackle the problem and make a fresh start in their life together.

The content of our worship can also speak to us. This may sound simple, even simplistic, but we can become so familiar with the format of our services, our minds become deadened to the truths God is wanting us to hear through them. We can easily sing a beloved hymn without really appreciating what we are singing. One morning, a few years ago, I was singing a song that I had sung many times before, about breaking chains and setting captives free, and it suddenly came to me – *yes*! That is what Jesus has done for me. I am no longer trapped in an unhappy situation. I am free to be a child of God, wherever I am.

Check it out

Some of us have experienced God speaking to us through the words of others, and some of us have not. Perhaps the most useful advice I can give is '*Listen*'. Too often we let our minds flit around like butterflies, thinking of anything but what the speaker is saying, or we are so eager to give our opinions we can hardly wait for the person to stop before we jump in with our own views. If you feel that something said in a sermon or by a friend has really touched your heart, write it down. Reflect on the last sermon you heard. Can you remember it? Was there anything there you found particularly striking? If you find you have forgotten what was said, perhaps you could make a few notes next time. If your church services are taped, why not get copies and listen in the peace and quiet of your home? If someone says something to you which has touched a raw spot or which might be meaningful, don't be defensive or evasive. Just tell them you need to pray about it and think it over. And you will need to check it out. Is what has been said to you biblical? Does it conform with what God has revealed of himself in the Bible? Does it lead us to Christ and give him the glory? Is it an answer to a prayer or problem? Is it relevant? And why not talk about the message with the person who brought it to you? How did it come to him or her? Is it just a wise observation? Did it arrive 'out of the blue'?

Satan can appear as an angel of light and his servants masquerade as servants of righteousness (2 Cor 11:14–15). What may appear to be wise counsel can be the counsel of deception. This does not mean, of course, that our friends or churches are messengers of Satan! But it is always wise to check out what people tell us, particularly those we don't know well. Any minister or pastor will want to talk to newcomers to the church to find out their Christian 'history'. Sadly, people are not always what they seem. Cults and fellowships which may appear to be Christian but which encourage their followers to cut themselves off from family and friends, to become exclusive, are particularly dangerous. They are destructive emotionally and spiritually, and doctrinally they are preaching a different gospel (2 Cor 11:4). What happened to the followers of David Koresh in 1993 at Waco, Texas, should serve as a tragic warning.

However God's message to us may come, we must not ignore it. It may require action, or a change of attitude on our part. We may need to pray, or to confess and ask forgiveness either of God or of someone we have hurt. And, through it all, we will see the power of life in God's words overflow in our lives, changing us in ways we could never have imagined and leading us on to new blessings and new experiences as his kingdom comes.

A word aptly spoken
  is like apples of gold in settings of silver.

(Proverbs 25:11)

Chapter 9

WORDS FROM OUTSIDE, WORDS FROM INSIDE

God speaks to us in the Bible, giving instruction, encouragement, comfort, guidance. He speaks to us through dreams, visions and pictures. He speaks to us in pain and suffering, as well as in joyful celebration. He speaks to us softly, with words that are personal, intimate and absolutely right for a particular situation. He speaks to us in a voice that thunders in our ears, when there is no need for interpretation or prayer for understanding. We may have absolutely no trouble in hearing or understanding him. Our difficulty may be that we don't always want to hear what he says.

Teresa was a very young Christian. She was also very rebellious and knew in her heart that she was pursuing a relationship that was quite wrong. None of her prayers seemed to be answered, and she was getting more and more confused and frustrated. Life didn't seem to be going as she wanted. Where was all this joyful life with Jesus?

Finally, in desperation, she shouted at God, 'OK God, I give up! What do you want then?'

God's response was short, clearly audible and rocked her back on her heels. 'Obedience,' he said.

Peter had everything going for him – good job, big salary, expenses-paid trips abroad, nice house, flash car and a wife whom he felt suited his social position. What else could he want?

On a business trip to New York, he checked in at his hotel and went to bed. As he lay in the dark trying to get to sleep, he suddenly heard a voice: 'Your wife is messing around with another man.'

Peter sat up in bed and switched on the light. There was no one there. Perhaps he had dreamed it. He turned off the light and lay down again.

Once more the voice said, 'Your wife is messing around with another man.'

Peter turned the light on again. Still no one there.

This time he felt very uneasy. 'What's going on here?' he thought. 'This is spooky.'

In the morning he tried to find a church, with the vague idea of asking about his supernatural experience. But the church was closed. He decided to get home as soon as possible and sort it out. On his return, he found that his wife had indeed left him for another man. What he thought was permanent in his life had gone and what he had thought important was valueless.

He cornered one of his colleagues at work. 'You're a Christian, aren't you? I want to see the bloke in charge at your church. Something's going on that I don't understand.'

Peter came to church and subsequently became a Christian. He was never in any doubt that the voice he heard was supernatural, and was indeed God.

Loud and clear

Anton is an architect. When his long-term business partner decided to move on, Anton found himself, for the first time, able to offer his business to the Lord to use for his kingdom. This he did, and a few weeks later he was shaken to hear a loud voice speak these words: 'Go, build my barns, for the harvest of the Lord is coming, and all the storehouses cannot contain that which I shall give.'

At the time there was not much feeling of revival in the air, but Anton waited expectantly for God to show him what to do. Five years on, his practice is handling several projects for churches whose 'storehouses' are not big enough for the 'harvest'. Bigger, 300-seater churches and large 1000-seater 'barns' are all under way. Anton knew that God had not asked him to 'do all this for free', but he felt that since he had offered his business to the Lord, he could not charge for kingdom work. His trust in God's provision for him has not been misplaced. In fact, Anton's financial director has been so impressed at God's handling of the finances, he too has become a Christian!

The experience of hearing God actually speak to you is unforgettable. His voice is loud, commanding, authoritative and imperative. There is no way anyone can mistake this for the gentle whisper spoken to Elijah (1 Kings 19:11–12). I have no doubt that it was God who spoke to me as a young Christian and told me to 'Read the Bible'. Teresa, Peter and Anton have no doubt at all that it was God speaking to them.

When Saul heard the voice of God thunder at him,

'Saul, Saul, why do you persecute me?' (Acts 9:4), it needed another person, Ananias, to hear God's voice before Saul's conversion could be consolidated by his baptism and receiving of the Holy Spirit. Ananias was understandably nervous at going to see the man whose persecution of Christians was notorious; but God said, 'Go', and Ananias went.

Paul heard God's voice and Ananias was the confirmation. I heard God's voice and discovered the true value of knowing the Bible (Rom 15:4; 2 Tim 3:16). Teresa heard God's voice and understood what she needed to do in her life (John 14:23). Peter heard God's voice and, as a result, gave his life to Jesus as his Lord and Saviour, rejecting the values of the society which he had previously adhered to (Rom 12:2). Anton heard God's voice giving him precise instructions for his business, and he carried them out (Psalm 32:8). For us all, there was no doubt that this was God speaking.

In our minds

God can also speak to us in a 'silent voice', deep within our minds, though we will be as aware of what he has said as if he had spoken aloud.

One year, my husband and I went for a short winter holiday in Madeira. It is a beautiful island and, even in February, it was as warm as an English summer. The Madeirans love flowers and produce spectacular displays in hotels, restaurants and public buildings. I was particularly fascinated by the 'Bird of Paradise' flower, with its fantastic purple 'beak' and orange 'feathered crest'. I longed to touch it, but there were always too many people around. Then we came across a mass of them growing in the flower beds round the entrance to the Lido, and I managed to get a sneaky feel. I was absolutely astonished at how stiff and unbending they were – they felt totally unlike any flower I knew. Then I heard God say to me, 'I can't use anyone like that.' For the rest of our week, these words went round and round my head. Was I being stiff and rigid? Were there ways in which I was not submitting to God's leading, wanting to go my own way or lacking in humility in my relationships with others? I had a lot to think about for some time afterwards.

During the Second World War, when Crete fell to the German forces, Wing Commander Edward Howell, who was later awarded the OBE and DFC, was badly wounded and captured. He was eventually sent to a prison camp in Salonika in northern Greece, where he became a Christian. Despite his wounds, he felt sure that God wanted him to escape. Now many of us in a similar situation would have wanted to escape too and we might probably have put Howell's feelings that it was God's desire that he escape down to wishful thinking. But Howell was right – God did want him out. One day a voice in his head said quite plainly, 'Tonight, half an hour after dusk.' It turned out that God's timing was perfect and, at an hour when the guards would normally be milling around, everything was quiet. Howell walked out of the prison, got over the wire and set off on his journey to freedom. It was not an easy journey, but he trusted God completely and saw many answers to prayer during his incredible journey back to England.

Brenda had been a Christian for many years when she was diagnosed with breast cancer. She was surprised at the diagnosis, but not devastated. She refused the offered counselling, explaining that the Lord would take care of her. The counselling nurse and the doctors were amazed, explaining that patients normally reacted strongly to this news – running away, fainting, hitting out at them, driving at great speed... Brenda was so calm they could not believe their eyes.

A couple of days later, she went to church as usual. When one of the leaders asked if she was OK, Brenda replied that she was fine but then admitted her illness. He quickly set about getting the other leaders together to pray for her. By then the service was starting, so he told Brenda that they would pray for her afterwards. Towards the end of the service, as the congregation waited on the Holy Spirit, God spoke into Brenda's mind, giving her a picture of a large, cupped hand, and saying, 'I have held you in the palm of my hand all your life. I will not let you go now. I will uphold you.'

Tears filled Brenda's eyes as she thanked her heavenly Father for his love and care. At the end of the meeting she said to the leaders that they did not need to pray for her. She told them what God had said and shown to her. She had never felt so uplifted. This feeling stayed with her throughout the operation to remove the cancer and subsequent radiation treatment. Six years later, she is still completely free from cancer. God's special word to Brenda was confirmed by his promises in Isaiah 41:10, which are always true.

Little words, long words

Throughout the Bible we read how the prophets and others heard God speak clearly to them. (We don't know exactly how they heard God, although it may well have been as the 'silent voice'.) And God spoke to them in a variety of ways, sometimes only briefly, with a few short words, and at other times at great length, in a fairly substantial conversation.

Jonah received brief instructions from God and, later on, some equally terse rebukes; but Isaiah and Jeremiah both received long prophecies (though we don't know if what is written was actually spoken all at the same time!). Isaiah received prophecies that could be quite poetic (eg Isaiah 31) or that could only be fully understood in the light of the birth, death and resurrection of Jesus (eg Isaiah 53). Jeremiah had words of condemnation and warnings of what would happen if God's words were ignored (eg Jer 9). Joshua was given precise instructions as he led the Israelites into the Promised Land and overcame the tribes there (Josh 1).

The morning after her father's death, Meg had woken early. As she lay thinking about him, her tears flowing, she started having all sorts of doubts in her mind, as so many of us do when faced with the realities of death. 'Is there really an afterlife? Is Dad in paradise now? Will I really see him again?'

Then Meg heard God speaking to her, showing her

the answers to these unspoken questions. She found herself thinking of a life that started from the end and worked backwards. She was in heaven and it was perfect. Then she was told that she was going down into the world.

'What's the world like?' she asked.

'It's a beautiful place. The people there have amazing physical bodies which are really quite miraculous in the way they are made. They do all sorts of different jobs, in factories, hospitals, schools and government. There are many creative people who paint beautiful pictures and write wonderful stories. There are musicians who play all kinds of instruments, producing delightful music. There are great oceans, massive mountains, rivers, lush countryside. Rain helps the crops to grow. The sun gives light and warmth. At night you can see the wonderful, jewel-like stars and the moon.'

'I can't believe it,' Meg said. 'It sounds hard to imagine.'

'Nevertheless, it is true,' she was told.

Life and all we have here is truly miraculous. Because of Meg's belief that God created her and the wonderful world around her, she could also believe that there was a heaven and one day she would be there with her heavenly Father. Through this she received tremendous peace.

Are they different?

What is different about all these people who have heard God? Why have they heard him so clearly, while others have not heard him speak at all?

One of the common factors seems to be their complete confidence that it is God speaking, along with their trust that he has matters well under control. No one has tried to add anything, to formulate 'plan B' in case God doesn't 'come up with the goods'. They have been obedient where obedience has been required. Teresa and Anton both did what God was asking of them. Brenda had so much confidence in him that she didn't react in the way the doctors thought she would. Neither, it is important to note, did she assume that God would heal her without medical intervention: God had said he would 'uphold' her, not 'heal' her, and she took him at his word.

So many of us, when we hear God's voice, prefer to make our own plans according to how we see the problem. It is easy to convince ourselves that what we want is what God wants! It is easy to pray about a situation and expect to see God act as we want him to. When we do not get the expected response, we assume that our prayers have not been answered at all.

Alarm bells

At this point a word of warning needs to be given. Many people hear voices, especially in their heads, but these are not from God. There may be a number of reasons for this.

- They may be our own desires and wishes.

- They may come from Satan.

- It is just possible they may be due to a psychiatric illness.

It is vitally important to say again, and this cannot be stressed too strongly, that we should check out what we think we are hearing. Is it biblical? Does it bring glory to God? Is it telling you to do something for the sole purpose of increasing your status, making you look good or increasing your wealth by dubious means? Is it asking you to do something which is not in accordance with Jesus' command that we love one another as he loved us (John 15:12)? Does it fit with God's principles of justice and mercy? Would you be happy to discuss what you have heard with a trusted Christian friend or your minister? Is it something you can share openly with others? We may well be prompted to do good things in secret (Matt 6:3–4), but we will never be asked to do bad things in secret.

If the answer to any of these questions is 'No', then the message you have heard is not from God. If you continue to hear the same voice giving you doubtful instructions or advice, you would be wise to seek medical advice or to consult your minister.

Hearing from God is an awesome experience. When he speaks out loud, we can be shaken to our very foundations. When he speaks 'silently' in our minds, it can be equally overwhelming. When Teresa and I were young Christians and heard God shout at us, we had no need to ask anyone if we had heard God. What he said to us had 'biblical' written all over it! Our problem, like countless others who have heard from God, was putting what he said into practice.

We may, like Jonah, prefer not to hear, and set off in the opposite direction. But when God has really spoken to us, his words will echo round our minds until we take them on board and do something about them. We may need to take some action, let go in trust or simply be prepared to wait. He may give us words of comfort or healing. But his words are always for our ultimate benefit. The psalmist knew this when he wrote, 'Your word is a lamp to my feet and a light for my path' (Psalm 119:105). We too can share in the illumination God's words bring to us.

Chapter 10

AND FINALLY...

It would be a very strange father who said to his son or daughter, 'Right! You just carry on with your life. I'll just stand back and see how you get on.' A really loving father wants to be involved with his children, talk to them, listen to them, guide and protect them, be part of their lives. Sadly, of course, there are fathers who do not act like this, but our heavenly Father is the perfect father who wants to have a close relationship with us. And part of his way of developing this relationship is to communicate with us.

Hopefully, by now some of the many ways in which God speaks to us will become more and more familiar to us as we open our ears and eyes expectantly. I believe that God is talking to us all the time. He says, 'Look at my creation. Isn't it wonderful? Look at those clouds, that sunrise, that mass of flowers. Aren't they beautiful?' Or he says, ' Look at the suffering, the starving, the dispossessed, the sick and bereaved. How will you show them my compassion?' Or he says, 'Look at the cruel, the greedy, the exploiters. How will you convince them of my anger at their injustice?'

He has shown you, O man, what is good.
  And what does the Lord require of you?
To act justly and to love mercy
  and to walk humbly with your God.

(Micah 6:8)

You have probably heard God more often than you
realise. He will challenge you in different ways as you
mature and develop your spiritual insight and understanding of him.

Different gifts

God has made us all different, physically, mentally
and temperamentally. He gives us different gifts and
he speaks to us in different ways. (It would be a very
boring world if we were all clones of each other!)

One day I was thinking about the gifts God gives
us, and rather wishing I had different gifts, when God
spoke to me, giving me a picture. He not only made
me laugh, but also made me thankful that he knows
what I need. I saw a big wooden table with a dozen
children sitting around the sides. They ranged from
grown teenagers down to a pair of toddlers. There
were six boys on one side and six girls on the other.
At the head was their father. It was Christmas and the
father was giving a present to each child. Each present was flat, wrapped in brown paper with a big red
ribbon tied round it. The children eagerly unwrapped
them. To their surpise, they discovered that they had
each been given a pair of adult-sized nylon tights!
The boys looked disgusted and the toddlers bewildered. Only the two teenage girls looked pleased.

Then I heard God say, 'I do not give the same gifts to all my children, just as an earthly father does not give the same gifts to his children.'

God does not give us all the same gifts; neither does he speak to all of us in exactly the same way. He knows us, how we will best hear him and respond to him. Just as the apostle Paul exhorts us to ask for other gifts (1 Cor 12:27–31), so God will challenge us to be adventurous and ready to listen to him in ways that may feel a bit strange to us. Hearing God can be exciting, even frightening. This is as it should be: 'The fear of the Lord is the beginning of wisdom' (Psalm 111:10). If we hear him with awe, respect and reverence (which is what is meant by the word 'fear'), then we will pay attention, listen and learn.

I did hear from God, once

Perhaps you have heard from God. Maybe you were at one of the big 'Bible Weeks', an evening of 'refreshing' or some other Christian jamboree, and you heard God speak to you. But when you got home and all the boring old details of ordinary life came back into focus, you never heard God again and are actually wondering whether you ever did. You may be thinking, 'Perhaps I didn't really hear God at all? Was it all just a load of emotional hype? What am I doing wrong? What was so different about that occasion?' All these questions are perfectly valid. Let's take a look at each of them.

'Perhaps I didn't hear God at all?'
Well, perhaps you didn't. Maybe what you thought

you heard was your own imagination or wishful thinking. But perhaps you did. Does it conform with our check-list? Do you think it was from God? (Be honest – no one is listening!) Did you hear from God but push what he said out of your mind because you didn't want to obey him? If that is the case, you know the answer. (Take heart, you are not the only one!)

'Was it just a load of emotional hype?'
There is a lot of emotional hype at some of these Christian events and, yes, some worship leaders can 'wind up' their audience. Check what you think God was saying to you with other mature Christians, especially the people who accompanied you to the event. Do they have any reservations about the occasion? If you are still uneasy about what went on, then tell God how you feel and ask him to speak to you again. We are all different and what one person finds spiritually uplifting, another finds all too emotional.

'What am I doing wrong?'
Well, *are* you doing anything wrong? What's going on in your life at the moment? Are you happy with it? Could you give God more of your time and attention? Is your mind preoccupied with other things, such as your problems, your status, unhelpful relationships, finances or other material concerns? Take time to do a spiritual health check on yourself.

'What was so different about that occasion?'
This is probably the most vital question. What *was* different? Was there plenty of praise and worship? Did

everyone humbly and thoughtfully bring themselves into God's presence? Did the leaders ask the Holy Spirit to come and fill those present?

> Enter his gates with thanksgiving
>   and his courts with praise;
> give thanks to him and praise his name.
>
> *(Psalm 100:4)*

We need to come into God's presence full of praise and thanksgiving. Perhaps a good way to 'enter his gates' is to come into his presence at the beginning of each day, praising, worshipping and giving thanks. Reading a praise psalm, such as Psalm 93, or making one of the psalms personal to you, eg Psalm 103 or 139; saying, ' I, John', or 'I, Sue', is a good way to start. Then ask God to help you hear his voice as the day unfolds.

One of my favourite walks takes me along an old road no longer used by cars and other traffic. At a couple of points on the way there are two old milestones. They are nearly hidden by ferns and wild plants; the letters and figures chiselled into the stone are covered with moss and lichens. Sometimes God's words are like that: we easily miss them as we rush by; they are hidden by our anxieties, false expectations and the demands of the world. Yet at other times his word is like a motorway direction sign – big, bright and there for all to see.

There are many ways in which we can hear God's voice and many places where he will speak to us. We do not need to be alone, very spiritual or even very quiet. God *will* speak to us and we will hear him, if we just listen with expectation and trust.

> In the silence of the stars,
> In the quiet of the hills,
> In the heaving of the sea,
> Speak, Lord.
>
> In the stillness of this room,
> In the calming of my mind,
> In the longing of my heart,
> Speak, Lord.
>
> In the voice of a friend,
> In the chatter of a child,
> In the words of a stranger,
> Speak, Lord.
>
> In the opening of a book,
> In the looking at a film,
> In the listening to music,
> Speak, Lord,
>
> For your servant listens.

('Speak Lord' by David Adam, from Tides and Seasons, Modern prayers in the Celtic tradition, *1989, Triangle Books, SPCK. Used with permission.)*

BIBLIOGRAPHY

Corrie Ten Boom, *Tramp for the Lord*, Hodder and Stoughton and CLC, 1974.

Gordon D Fee and Douglas Stuart, *How to read the Bible for all its Worth*, Scripture Union, 1994.

Jane Grayshon, *A Harvest of Pain*, Kingsway, 1989; *A Pathway through Pain* (1995), and *Treasures of Darkness* (1996), Hodder & Stoughton.

Jennifer Rees Larcombe, *God's Gloves*, Marshall Pickering, 1987; *Beyond Healing* (1986), and *Unexpected Healing* (1991), Hodder and Stoughton.

Wing Commander Edward Howell, OBE, DFC, *Escape to Live*, Grosvenor, 1981.

OTHER TITLES FROM SCRIPTURE UNION

Through the Bible in a Year: A spiritual journal
Dennis Lennon
A completely original syllabus, constructed around eleven themes, gives an overarching picture of the whole Bible story. There is space for the reader to keep a written record of their spiritual journey.
1 85999 196 3, £9.99

How to Read the Bible for all its Worth (2nd ed)
Gordon D Fee and Douglas Stuart
This in-depth Bible reading guide is consistently popular and fast becoming a classic.
0 86201 974 5, £7.50

Be an Expert (in 137 minutes) in Interpreting the Bible
Richard Briggs
A short, entertaining and informative guide to biblical interpretation (hermeneutics). With humour and clarity, Richard Briggs outlines biblical genre and other difficult concepts in a way that ordinary people can understand.
1 85999 224 2, £3.99

Life's Like That: Meeting God in the everyday
Jeanette Henderson
Brimming with warmth and humour, these anecdotes offer a fresh perspective on selected Bible passages. The author draws on her experiences of family life in this country, and short-term missions in Africa, to show how we can learn to see God at work in the ups and down of everyday life.
1 85999 311 7, £4.99

Closer to God: Practical help on your spiritual journey
Ian Bunting (ed)
We're all on a journey through life, with God. For many it is a struggle. What may help us? In this book, members of the Grove Spirituality Group write from personal experience, and from their understanding of the way Christians have come closer to God down the centuries.
0 86201 550 2, £5.99

How to Pray When Life Hurts
Roy Lawrence
Prayer makes a difference because God makes a difference. Whether we feel guilty or angry, fearful or under pressure, this book offers practical help on how to pray when life hurts.
0 86201 969 9, £5.99

Make Me a Channel
Roy Lawrence
This book highlights the struggle many Christians

have in achieving the balance between receiving from God and giving to others. But we need to do both to be any good at either. Without God's input, our good intentions flounder; but if we don't share his gifts, we are not being the people he wants us to be.

1 85999 015 0, £4.99

Walking Backwards: Dealing with guilt
Jeff Lucas

Are you struggling with things you've repented of but can't forget? It is God's will for you to turn, face the future and leave the past finally and completely behind. Written in a lively, anecdotal style, this is a down-to-earth book on forgiveness.

0 86201 973 7, £4.99

Weak Enough for God to Use
Dennis Lennon

Biblical inspiration for Christians, to encourage them to believe that God uses ordinary people to do mighty things for him. Includes character studies of Mary, Moses, David, Jeremiah among others, as well as contemporary accounts of people who have made an impact on the world around them.

1 85999 290 0, £4.99

Finding a Spiritual Friend
Timothy Jones

Every Christian needs the support, direction and encouragement that comes with meaningful spiritual friendship. This inspirational guide shows the reader how to go about establishing these relationships,

drawing on the author's personal experience and a combination of biblical examples, classical writings, contemporary stories and guidance on prayer.
1 85999 336 2, £4.99

Spiritual Encounter Guides
Stephen D and Jacalyn Eyre
A fresh approach to personal devotion for new or long-time Christians, the aim of these Bible studies is to help readers find intimacy with God. Each book contains one month's Bible reading material. £3.50 each.
Abiding in Christ's Love, 1 85999 021 5
Sinking Your Roots in Christ, 1 8 5999 022 3
Sitting at the Feet of Jesus, 1 85999 020 7
Waiting on the Lord, 1 85999 019 3

Tune In
A superb concept in audio cassettes, clips from the Bible and contemporary Christian music blend with the voices of well-known Christians and ordinary people to bring a fresh perspective to key Bible texts. Easy listening for car journeys, or a thought-provoking opener for quiet times or group Bible studies. Both double cassette packages, £8.99 each.
Tune in to the Beatitudes, 1 85999 092 4
Tune in to the Fruit of the Spirit, 1 85999 093 2

All these titles are available from your local Christian bookshop, or from SU Mail Order, PO Box 764, Oxford, OX4 5FJ; tel (01865) 716880, fax (01865) 715152.

For a complete catalogue of resources from Scripture Union, please contact SU Sales and Promotions, 207-209 Queensway, Bletchley, Milton Keynes, MK2 2EB; tel (01908) 856000, fax (01908) 856111.